Travel Behaviour Reconsidered in an
Era of Decarbonisation

Travel Behaviour Reconsidered in an Era of Decarbonisation

David Metz

First published in 2024 by
UCL Press
University College London
Gower Street
London WC1E 6BT

Available to download free: www.uclpress.co.uk

Text © Author, 2024
Images © Copyright holders named in captions, 2024

The author has asserted his rights under the Copyright, Designs and Patents Act 1988 to be identified as the author of this work.

A CIP catalogue record for this book is available from The British Library.

Any third-party material in this book is not covered by the book's Creative Commons licence. Details of the copyright ownership and permitted use of third-party material is given in the image (or extract) credit lines. If you would like to reuse any third-party material not covered by the book's Creative Commons licence, you will need to obtain permission directly from the copyright owner.

This book is published under a Creative Commons Attribution-Non-Commercial 4.0 International licence (CC BY-NC 4.0), https://creativecommons.org/licenses/by-nc/4.0/. This licence allows you to share and adapt the work for non-commercial use providing attribution is made to the author and publisher (but not in any way that suggests that they endorse you or your use of the work) and any changes are indicated. Attribution should include the following information:

Metz, D. 2024. *Travel Behaviour Reconsidered in an Era of Decarbonisation*. London: UCL Press. https://doi.org/10.14324/111.9781800087163

Further details about Creative Commons licences are available at https://creativecommons.org/licenses/

ISBN: 978-1-80008-718-7 (Hbk.)
ISBN: 978-1-80008-717-0 (Pbk.)
ISBN: 978-1-80008-716-3 (PDF)
ISBN: 978-1-80008-719-4 (epub)
DOI: https://doi.org/10.14324/111.9781800087163

Contents

List of figures and tables	vii
List of abbreviations	ix
Preface	xi
1 Travel behaviour today	1
2 Travel trends over time	15
3 Shock of the pandemic	31
4 Transport economics reconsidered	41
5 Transport models reconsidered	93
6 Demands of decarbonisation	111
7 Fresh approaches to travel analysis and policy	135
References	147
Index	159

List of figures and tables

Figures

1.1	Travel mode share in England 2019.	2
1.2	Trip mode share in 2018, Copenhagen and London.	6
2.1	Average travel distance, time and trips per person per year in Britain.	16
2.2	Rail passenger numbers in Britain 1830–2021.	18
2.3	Share of travel by car, trains and buses in Britain.	28
3.1	Average weekly demand on London's transport networks compared to the equivalent week before the pandemic.	32

Tables

3.1	Average annual number of trips, distance travelled and travel time in England, 2019–22.	39

List of abbreviations

AV	Autonomous vehicle
BCR	Benefit–cost ratio
CO_2	Carbon dioxide
CGE	Computable general equilibrium [models]
BEV	Battery electric vehicle
DfT	Department for Transport (UK)
ETS	Emission trading scheme
EV	Electric vehicle
FCEV	Fuel cell electric vehicle
GHG	Greenhouse gases
GPS	Global Positioning System
HGV	Heavy goods vehicle
HS2	High Speed 2
ICEV	Internal combustion engine vehicle
ITF	International Transport Forum
LUTI	Land use and transport interaction [models]
MaaS	Mobility as a service
MAC	Marginal abatement cost
MtCO2e	Million tonnes of CO_2 equivalent
NAO	National Audit Office
NTM	National Transport Model
NTEM	National Trip End Model
NTS	National Travel Survey
PHEV	Plug-in hybrid electric vehicle
RIS3	Road investment strategy 3
RP	Revealed preference
SACTRA	Standing Advisory Committee on Trunk Road Assessment
SAF	Sustainable aviation fuel
SP	Stated preference
SUV	Sports utility vehicle
TAG	Transport Analysis Guidance

TfL	Transport for London
VTTS	Value of travel time saving
WTP	Willingness to pay
ZEV	Zero-emission vehicle

List of abbreviations

AV	Autonomous vehicle
BCR	Benefit–cost ratio
CO_2	Carbon dioxide
CGE	Computable general equilibrium [models]
BEV	Battery electric vehicle
DfT	Department for Transport (UK)
ETS	Emission trading scheme
EV	Electric vehicle
FCEV	Fuel cell electric vehicle
GHG	Greenhouse gases
GPS	Global Positioning System
HGV	Heavy goods vehicle
HS2	High Speed 2
ICEV	Internal combustion engine vehicle
ITF	International Transport Forum
LUTI	Land use and transport interaction [models]
MaaS	Mobility as a service
MAC	Marginal abatement cost
MtCO2e	Million tonnes of CO_2 equivalent
NAO	National Audit Office
NTM	National Transport Model
NTEM	National Trip End Model
NTS	National Travel Survey
PHEV	Plug-in hybrid electric vehicle
RIS3	Road investment strategy 3
RP	Revealed preference
SACTRA	Standing Advisory Committee on Trunk Road Assessment
SAF	Sustainable aviation fuel
SP	Stated preference
SUV	Sports utility vehicle
TAG	Transport Analysis Guidance

TfL	Transport for London
VTTS	Value of travel time saving
WTP	Willingness to pay
ZEV	Zero-emission vehicle

Preface

Why we travel, how we travel, where we travel and how much we travel: these are central concerns of modern life, as are the impacts that travel has on our environment. It's all quite complicated, involving a number of strands of thought and intellectual disciplines ranging from human behaviour through to civil engineering. Understanding causal relationships sufficiently to make useful improvements is therefore not easy. Yet this area of 'transport studies', as it is usually designated, is very much an applied science, where knowledge for its own sake has limited value. What is needed are insights based on evidence that have sufficient validity to justify interventions to improve the experience of users of the transport system and to reduce its impact of the environment.

Accordingly, it is necessary to ask two questions, in sequence: first, what's going on here? And when that is answered adequately, the second question is: what can we do to improve matters? Analysis before advocacy. This book is my latest in a series of books and papers aimed at a variety of audiences, intended to address these questions in the light of continuing developments of transport technologies and policies, most recently and importantly the need to decarbonise the transport system to meet climate change objectives. A fuller list of my publications will be found in the References, but here I might mention the two most recent books: *Driving Change: Travel in the twenty-first century* (Metz 2019), which focused on the new transport technologies, and *Good to Go? Decarbonising travel after the pandemic* (Metz 2022a), which addressed the challenge of responding to climate change in light of the initial experience of the coronavirus pandemic. These books were aimed at both transport practitioners and those concerned with transport policy. A subsidiary theme was a critique of the orthodox approach to the economic analysis of transport investments, for which the main benefit is supposed to be the value of travel time saved through travelling faster. This new book brings this critique to the fore, pointing up the inconsistency with the empirical observation that average travel time is a long run invariant.

I was more appreciative of this inconsistency than many academics and practitioners through having come to the field of transport studies in a circuitous route that did not include any formal training in the discipline. I started out with a doctorate in biophysics and a decade of biomedical research, following which I switched to policy advice in central government, mainly in the Energy Department, subsequently taking the post of Chief Scientist at the Department for Transport. After 20 years in Whitehall departments, I left the civil service, initially leading a project to stimulate ageing research across the disciplines, then to focus on the relationship between mobility and the quality of later life, and most recently to study mobility as seen through travel behaviour and the functioning of the transport system. When in the Energy Department, I learned about cost–benefit analysis, and when I moved to the Department for Transport, I saw how time savings were assumed to be the main economic benefit of investment in new transport facilities. Yet at the same time, there was an emerging stream of data on travel behaviour indicating that average travel time for settled human populations changed little over the years, despite huge expenditure on transport investments, justified largely by the saving of travel time. The inference was that people were taking the benefits of such investment to travel further, to increase access to people, places, services and activities, with the ensuing enhancement of opportunities and choices.

For many years I have been pointing to the inconsistency between the supposition of travel time savings and the observation of improved access, in both peer-reviewed papers and books. The core of this new book is a full articulation of my critique, aimed at researchers and professionals who are concerned with the foundations of transport investment analysis. But this is not merely a matter of academic interest since many billions of pounds are spent by national and local government each year on adding to transport infrastructure capacity, justified largely by the saving of travel time. I will argue that much of this spend is misdirected on account of a misconceived economic framework.

The focus of this book is travel and transport in the United Kingdom for a number of reasons. The UK Department for Transport is world leading in the breadth and depth of the travel and transport statistics that it publishes. London is also world leading in the travel statistics published annually for the city region. And because I live in London and have first-hand knowledge, I am able to associate data with causation with more confidence than would be possible for other cities and countries. Nevertheless, relevant findings are citied from other developed economies, where the same issues and challenges are being addressed, allowing for different geographies, population densities and path dependences.

This book is primarily concerned with personal travel. Yet roads, railways and airports are shared with vehicles delivering freight, for which useful data are more limited, although all users of transport systems contribute to carbon emissions, air pollution, congestion and other externalities. And there can be competition for space between personal travellers and freight deliveries, as will be discussed.

The first chapter outlines travel behaviour as it is today, particularly the dominance of the car as an effective means of meeting mobility needs, yet with many associated detriments, of which carbon emissions from the use of oil-based fuels has become of central importance. Chapter 2 sets out the historical trends in travel behaviour, notably the growth in distance travelled as car ownership grew, while average travel time remained fixed at about an hour a day. However, this growth of per capita car use ceased around the turn of the century, the consequence of both exhausting the possibilities for faster travel and saturation of demand for travel. Chapter 3 summarises the impact of the coronavirus pandemic on travel behaviour and the general reversion to previous travel patterns, indicating that while our travel behaviour could change substantially under the impetus of concerns for personal health, this is not our preference.

Chapter 4 of this book is its core, a critique of the orthodox approach of transport economists and governments to investment appraisal, together with discussion of alternatives. This chapter is the longest in the book, in part because there proved to be no natural point at which to create a break. Depending on their interests and prior knowledge, readers may not wish to consider all the aspects discussed, so judicious skipping of sections, as signposted at the beginning of the chapter, would not detract from the understanding of subsequent chapters.

Chapter 5 is a critique of the validity of conventional transport modelling, where the outputs of conventional models are inputs to economic analysis that suppose time savings to be the main benefit.

Chapter 6 discusses the demands of transport-sector decarbonisation, a high-level strategic policy requirement, considering the prospects for both technological and behavioural change. The orthodox supposition that travel demand growth is inexorable, requiring continued investment in additional transport capacity is challenged in Chapter 7, where it is argued that the transport network is largely mature, with the need to make most effective use of existing assets as a central element of policy going forward. This allows the problematic economic analysis of new investment to be relegated in importance, to be replaced with the operational analysis of transport networks to improve the efficiency of existing assets.

The approach summarised above runs contrary to that developed over the past half-century by transport economists. The pioneers of the field were influential with policymakers since cost–benefit analysis could be used both to help prioritise transport investments and to make a persuasive case to the finance department (HM Treasury in the UK) that funds would be well spent. The Department for Transport's implementation of cost–benefit analysis was seen by the Treasury as well exemplifying the desired general approach to valuing public expenditure, as set out in successive editions of its 'Green Book' on appraisal and evaluation in central government. This assisted the Department for Transport when bidding for funds in competition with other government departments. In recent years very substantial funding for investment in both road and rail has been allocated, in line with the general desire of politicians, both national and local, to announce new schemes that it is hoped will reduce congestion, improve connectivity and boost economic growth. However, as will be argued in this volume, such hopes have largely proved nugatory, for reasons that can be understood.

Regrettably, the critique that I have developed has been substantially a single-handed effort, at least among those in academia and elsewhere who are free to publish in the research journals. On the other hand, surveys of transport planners, who are largely employed in local government and in consultancies, find a substantial desire for major reform of the conventional approach. The failure of transport economists to undertake critical reappraisal and introduce fresh thinking is disappointing, perhaps the consequence of the retirement of the pioneers and lack of attraction of the sub-discipline for innovative new entrants. Besides, transport economics has substantially operated in a silo, distinct from the adjacent disciplines of spatial economics and operations research. And the scope of transport studies as an academic subject has not developed helpfully, as far as critical application to policy and investment decisions is concerned.

The research literature – papers on aspects of travel and transport in peer-reviewed journals – has burgeoned in recent years. There are many more papers in established journals and in new journals that have been created, often on an open-access basis whereby the researchers pay the cost of publication, rather than journals relying on libraries taking out subscriptions. There may therefore be an incentive to relax standards in the peer-review process to generate more income, lessening the overall quality of the research literature, which accords with my subjective impression.

One feature of many recent publications is the theoretical modelling of a new technology. This may be useful where there is a clear practical need, for instance the optimal deployment of charging points for electric vehicles.

Yet there is also extensive modelling activity in relation to the deployment of autonomous vehicles (AVs), where experience of on-road behaviour is extremely limited thus far. Because model outputs depend on assumptions about AV performance parameters, the conclusions of such studies are very varied and provide little in the way of useful guidance to practitioners and policymakers. Theoretical development of models seems an objective in itself, justified by a vague hope that this might be of practical use were further research to be carried out and more extensive data collected.

Another feature of the literature is the excessively formal analysis of survey findings, for instance of the responses to surveys of the expected impact of a new technology, such as AVs, whether of drivers or city planners. Yet rarely are findings reported as charts, histograms or scatter diagrams, with uncertainty shown visually, which would make clear the common limited significance of most conclusions. In part, this may be due to the need of academics to publish for career success, even if the findings of research turn out to be of little practical value, as is commonly the case, and the willingness of journal editors and reviewers to recognise this motivation.

A further feature of the recent literature is the systematic review, in which formal search methodologies are employed to identify all relevant papers on a topic. One problem is that because of the deteriorating quality of the literature, it becomes difficult to see the wood for the trees, as every paper needs to be cited. Systematic review originated in the medical literature where the aim of such meta-analysis is to identify every relevant study of a condition or treatment, with a ranking by quality such that only the highest-quality papers contribute to the conclusions of the review. But for transport studies, such quality ranking is not practical, in part because particular findings are commonly path dependent and specific to particular locations or circumstances – case studies rather than controlled trials. Hence it is difficult to distil empirical experience to yield useful heuristics to guide policy and practice. The result is reviews that commonly fail to illuminate the likely options for useful innovation.

For this reason, there has emerged the rapid evidence review, increasingly commissioned by government departments to draw swift conclusions from a selection of relevant research papers, but with the risk of bias in that selection, including the disregard of evidence that challenges preconceived conclusions.

I have noticed increasing reference in the recent literature to transport researchers as 'scholars', a term hitherto largely reserved for those working in the humanities. Generally, those involved in transport research had seen themselves as based in disciplines such as engineering, economics, planning and the environmental sciences.

The purpose of research within such disciplinary frameworks has been to advance understanding and thereby contribute to practical solutions to the problems of the transport sector. We have not, I think, seen ourselves as primarily involved in developing a branch of knowledge through scholarship that focuses on the extant literature. Indeed, the inward-looking processes of scholarship are filling the literature with findings of little use and thereby may be displacing contributions of more practical value, while often disregarding other sources of evidence such as official statistics and reports from government departments and non-governmental organisations.

Despite these shortcomings of the published research literature, in this volume I have cited extensive findings, both those consistent with my own perspective and those supportive of orthodox approaches, aiming to include all sources that are clear and relevant to the arguments developed.

Nevertheless, there remains a substantial disconnect between the needs of decision makers for evidence-based analytical support and what the academic transport economists, modellers and analysts are contributing to the progress of the field. In my view, the point of research in transport studies is not to advance the science of human behaviour, which is too multifaceted for a focus on one aspect to usefully illuminate. Nor is it to develop theory with little practical applicability. Rather, the need is for research that advances our ability to understand the complex interactions between travel behaviour and the transport system, and then to identify opportunities to make improvements. I hope this book may help remedy the deformations of transport research and assist practitioners in their tasks by proposing causal relationships in non-technical terms that are both relevant to policy and open to contention through the eliciting of fresh evidence.

This book was completed at the end of 2023. The matters discussed here continue to develop. I will comment on developments in my blog at http://drivingchange.org.uk and in shorter form at https://davidmetz. substack.com; the latter can be subscribed to without charge.

*

I am grateful for hospitality from colleagues at the UCL Centre for Transport Studies. I have appreciated the opportunity made possible by Peter Stonham, publisher of the estimable fortnightly *Local Transport Today*, of a regular column in which some of the ideas in this book have been given initial exposure. I thank Chris Penfold, Elliot Beck, Robert Davies and their colleagues at UCL Press for commissioning this book and taking it through to publication. Involvement with UCL has been particularly gratifying, as it is the institution in which I took my first degree.

1
Travel behaviour today

1.1 Introduction

This chapter will summarise the main features of travel behaviour in the United Kingdom prior to the coronavirus pandemic – why and how we travel – drawing largely on the findings of the exceptionally comprehensive UK National Travel Survey (the impact of the pandemic will be considered in Chapter 3). The UK is representative of developed economies in many respects, particularly the dominant role of car travel on account of this mode's efficiency in providing door-to-door travel where congestion is not too severe and where parking is available at both ends of the journey. However, there are differences between countries in how travel is made possible by the transport system, comprising the road and rail networks in cities, towns and beyond, plus the facilities for air travel, and these differences will be considered to the extent that comparable data is available in this and subsequent chapters.

There are a variety of detrimental consequences of travel using the transport system, including carbon emissions, urban air pollution, road traffic congestion, noise, adverse impacts on the natural environment, deaths and injuries, and traffic that impedes pedestrians and severs communities. We have become habituated to high levels of access made possible by the modern transport system, and have learned to tolerate the detriments while hoping for improvements. Accordingly, considerable efforts are being made to tackle these detriments, with carbon emissions an especial focus of effort, as will be discussed in Chapter 6.

1.2 Survey findings

The UK Department for Transport has for half a century commissioned a National Travel Survey (NTS), now conducted annually, generating an

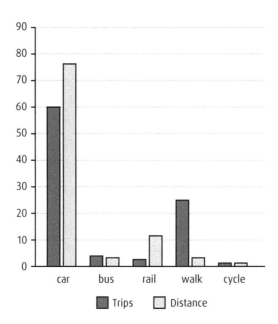

Figure 1.1 Travel mode share (%) in England 2019. Source: NTS table 0409. Taxi and other private transport omitted.

exceptionally long time series of travel behaviour findings. This covers personal travel within Great Britain, more recently in England only, by residents of private households, along the public highway, by rail or by air. (Scotland and Wales now carry out their own surveys.) Travel off-road or for commercial purposes is not included; nor is international travel by air. Some 14,000 individuals, chosen to represent the population as a whole, complete seven-day travel diaries, recording all their journeys. The travel trends over time will be considered in the next chapter. Here we take a snapshot drawn from the 2019 NTS report, the most recent prior to the coronavirus pandemic.

In 2019, averaged across the population, 953 trips per person per year were made, taking 370 hours (very close to an hour a day), covering 6,500 miles a year. The average journey length was 6.8 miles (NTS 2019, table 0101). Most of these journeys were for daily travel, but included also are the infrequent longer trips, for instance for holidays.

The car was the dominant mode of travel, responsible for 61 per cent of all trips and 77 per cent of total distance travelled, driver and passenger together (NTS 2019, table 0409). Seventy-six per cent of households owned at least one car (NTS 2019, table 0205). Eighty per cent of men aged 17 and over held a driving licence, and 71 per cent of women (NTS 2019, table 0201). A recent attitude survey found that 87 per cent of cars owners agreed, strongly or slightly, that their current lifestyle required ownership of a car and 95 per cent agreed that they enjoyed the freedom and independence this gave them (DfT 2019a). Another analysis of survey data found that 69 per cent of the population had personal access to a car and 87 per cent used a car at least once a week; and that personal car use was important for accessing employment, services and social participation (Chatterjee et al. 2019). In towns, as opposed to cities that have better public transport, around 80 per cent of commuting to work was by private transport (NIC 2021).

Compared to the car, the other motorised modes comprise a much smaller share of journeys nationally, as shown in Figure 1.1: buses are responsible for 5 per cent of trips and 4 per cent of distance; rail for only 3 per cent of trips but 12 per cent of distance. Of what are known as the 'active modes' (previously the 'slow modes'), walking is responsible for 26 per cent of trips but only 3 per cent of distance; and cycling for 1 per cent of trips and 1 per cent of distance (NTS 2019, table 0409).

The most common journey purpose was leisure, comprising 26 per cent of all trips, followed by shopping (19 per cent), commuting (15 per cent) and education (13 per cent); business travel was responsible for only 3 per cent of all journeys, although for 9 per cent of distance (NTS 2019, table 0409). Travel patterns vary with age: people in mid-life (age range 40–9) travel most (18 per cent more than the average); children and young people under age 20 travel less (12 per cent below average); and those over 70 travel least (16 per cent less than average) (NTS 2019, table 0601). Journey length varies with purpose, commuting trips being the longest at 31 minutes on average, while escorting children to school is the shortest at 14 minutes (NTS 2019, 0403).

There are significant differences in travel depending on geography, particularly for car use, which is responsible for 52 per cent of trips in urban conurbations as opposed to 78 per cent in rural villages and beyond. In London, car use is especially low, responsible for only 34 per cent of trips, in part a consequence of the extensive public transport system as well as traffic congestion and limited parking space (NTS 2019, table 9903). Car ownership runs in parallel: only 5 per cent of households own no car in rural villages, compared with 45 per cent in London (NTS 2019, table 9902). Household car availability varies with income, with 45 per cent of the lowest quintile not owning a car or van, compared with 14 per cent of the highest (NTS 2019, table 0703). There are also variations in average travel time for sub-groups. People living in urban areas spent 366 hours per person per year travelling on average, compared to 404 hours for those in rural villages (NTS 2019, table 9913). Earlier data showed that people in mid-life spent some 60 per cent more time travelling than children and older people, while people in the highest income quintile spent 70 per cent more time on the move than those in the lowest, a reflection of more active lifestyles (Metz 2005).

These data are cross-sectional, referring to travel behaviour at one point in time, immediately pre-pandemic; trends over time will be discussed in the next chapter. The figures are also averages for groups within the population. Within each group, there is a range of travel behaviour, from those who rarely leave home on account of disability, to the super commuters who travel considerable distances each day. The range reflects in part inequalities in society, of income, education and health, to be discussed later (section 1.6).

Beyond Britain, use of the different modes of travel varies quite widely, depending on both geography and history. North American cities that grew in the era of the automobile have high levels of car use while compact European cities like Amsterdam and Copenhagen are famous for large numbers of cyclists. This will be considered next.

1.3 Car dependence

An important feature of travel behaviour that emerges from the previous discussion is the high level of car use in the UK and other developed economies. The popularity of the car arose in the second half of the last century. In the 1950s, public transport was the more important travel mode, but the growth of car ownership led to reduced use of buses in particular and hence to the decline in bus services, a self-reinforcing process. Yet the dominance of the car is also the source of most of the current problems with the transport system.

The concept of car dependence was first articulated by Goodwin (1995), prompted by the observation that many people have built their way of life around their cars and depend on them for many regular and occasional journeys, despite the wide range of societal problems arising from growing car use. Goodwin noted the distinction between car-dependent people and car-dependent trips, suggesting that focus on the latter would be more likely to lead to changes in behaviour. Goodwin also recognised that car dependence is a process, not a state, such that those acquiring cars tend to rely on them more over time and pay less attention to alternatives.

The concept of car dependence has stimulated much academic research. The current critique of car ownership and use has a two-fold thrust: challenge to the existence of locations where the car is the only feasible means of access, particularly where other modes of travel might be provided; and challenge to car use in locations where other modes are available in the form of public transport and active travel. In this latter context, the term 'car dependence' has some resonance with other kinds of undesirable dependence, such as on alcohol or drugs (Metz 2023a). Nevertheless, the impact of the critique of car dependence on observed travel behaviour has been at best quite limited, as indicated by the high level of car use outlined above, more than two decades after the concept was first enunciated.

A new impetus to address car dependence arises from the need to decarbonise the surface transport sector, for which many analysts and policy advisors take the view that technological change, largely by replacing the internal combustion engine by electric propulsion, would in itself be insufficient to achieve a trajectory to Net Zero by 2050 consistent with international agreements. Thus, the intergovernmental International Transport Forum argues that reducing reliance on cars in cities is pivotal to decarbonise urban mobility (ITF 2021), a topic that will be considered fully in Chapter 6. Yet the attractions of the car work against such reduction.

So the question to be asked is why car dependence has generally persisted, despite analytical and policy orientations that favour its decline. In broad terms, the answer two-fold. First, the widespread deployment of the car over the past century has proceeded in parallel with the development of the built environment, within which are found the origins and destinations of nearly all trips. Expeditious door-to-door travel by car has made possible access to a wide range of people, services, activities and destinations to which we have become habituated. As with path-dependent processes generally, reversal is difficult without loss of benefit. Second, car ownership is attractive to a large proportion of the population, and a large industry has come into being to satisfy this desire. These two aspects will be discussed next.

1.3.1 Utility of the car

Copenhagen is a city famous for cycling, having excellent infrastructure and a strong cycling culture. As shown in Figure 1.2, 28 per cent of all trips to, from and within that city were made by bike in 2018 (City of Copenhagen 2019, 6). However, car mode share was 32 per cent, which

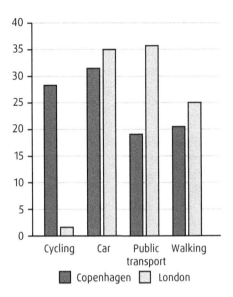

Figure 1.2 Trip mode share (%) in 2018, Copenhagen and London. Sources: City of Copenhagen (2018; data for trips to, from and in the city of Copenhagen) and Transport for London (2019; data for all trips by residents and non-residents with origin and destination or both in the area of the Greater London Authority; motorcycle and taxi omitted).

was only three percentage points less than in London (TfL 2019, Figure 2.3). Aside from cycling, the other large difference between the two cities is that public transport mode share in Copenhagen is half that of London, 19 per cent against 36 per cent respectively, a difference that is insufficiently recognised. This is consistent with the proposition that people can be attracted away from buses onto bicycles by good cycling facilities, since cycling is cheaper, healthier, environmentally benign and no slower than the bus in congested traffic. Yet the car remains attractive even in Copenhagen, a small, flat city, where almost all drivers have experience of safe cycling.

Some information on trip mode shares is available for other European cities. Kodukula et al. (2018) compiled data for 13 cities. A wide range of travel patterns was found, reflecting the location of historical city boundaries, population density and public transport provision. There were also differences in the sources of data, whether from household surveys or from counts of traffic and passengers. It was found that Amsterdam was similar to Copenhagen with 32 per cent cycling and 17 per cent public transport. In contrast, Vienna, Zurich and Madrid were similar to London with 38–40 per cent public transport, although rather more cycling (6–8 per cent). However, no city was found to have high levels of both cycling and public transport. Buehler at al. (2017) found that the largest cities in Austria, Switzerland and Germany had succeeded in reducing the car share of trips over the past 25 years: from 40 to 27 per cent in Vienna, from 40 to 33 per cent in Munich, from 35 to 30 per cent in Berlin, from 39 to 30 per cent in Zurich and from 48 to 42 per cent in Hamburg. Nevertheless, car use remains substantial, notwithstanding policies to reduce car dependence.

So why are cars widely used even in cities that encourage other modes of travel? The answer surely lies in the utility of cars, which are useful for carrying people and goods, including child seats and other pieces of equipment that are regularly used, as well as for making trips longer than would be comfortable by bicycle. The car is well suited for meeting needs for access to people and places, including for trips with a chain of destinations and for door-to-door travel where there is road space to drive without unacceptable congestion delays and the ability to park at both ends of the journey. Car travel generally requires less planning than trips by public transport, with digital navigation based on satnav devices a means of selecting the quickest route. The car offers flexibility, comfort, privacy and security, compared to public transport, particularly for people with mobility difficulties. The most common mode of travel for adults in England with a mobility difficulty was by car, with on average 238 trips per person per year as drivers and 178 as passengers, compared to 123 walking trips, 39 bus trips and 7 rail trips (NTS 2019, table 0709).

Car travel may feel less costly than public transport, particularly with a full load of passengers. Car ownership requires a commitment to pay the costs of purchase, servicing and insurance, so trading large one-off payments for low marginal costs at the time of use. Such sunk costs are largely disregarded when making a choice between car use, active travel and public transport for an intended trip. Thaler (1999), in his seminal paper on 'mental accounting', observes that many urban car owners would be financially better off selling their car and using a combination of taxis and car rentals; yet paying $10 to take a taxi to the supermarket or a movie is both salient and linked to the consumption act, so it seems to raise the price of groceries and movies in a way that monthly car payments or a fully owned car do not.

Importantly, the amount of travel that can be undertaken is limited by the time available, given the 24 hours of the day and all the activities that must be fitted in. For settled populations, average travel time amounts to about one hour a day, as will be discussed in the next chapter. Accordingly, faster travel allows greater access within the travel time available. Car travel is generally faster, door to door, than other modes over short to moderate distances, which increases people's access to desired destinations. Access increases approximately with the square of the speed of travel, so that urban car travel at, say, 30 km/h allows four times the access than does cycling at 15 km/h, and 36 times more than walking at 5 km/h.

The value of access to people, places, activities and services, of the choices and opportunities that ensue, is the main reason for the popularity of the car for short-to-medium-distance journeys where there is adequate road space, and for longer trips where the alternative modes, rail or air travel, may be less attractive. Yet the attractions of car ownership go beyond the utilitarian, as discussed next.

1.3.2 Attractions of car ownership

There is a literature on why the car is seen by many as attractive, quite apart from its utility for making journeys. Sheller (2004) argued that 'car consumption' is never simply about rational economic choices, but is as much about aesthetic, emotional and sensory responses to driving, as well as patterns of kinship, sociability, habitation and work. Steg (2005) noted motives for car ownership that included feelings of sensation, power, superiority, self-esteem and social status. She carried out interviews with samples of drivers to demonstrate that symbolic and affective motives play an important role in explaining the level of car use, in particular for commuting, concluding that these motives may be a reason why attempts to influence car use have not been very successful. Gatersleben (2021) has summarised the extensive yet diverse literature on the symbolic and affective aspects of car ownership and use. Cars can be symbols of social identity and status as well as of personal identity. Affective aspects refer to emotions that include pleasure and pride, freedom yet being in control, and in the exercise of driving skills.

Moody and Zhao (2019) developed a survey methodology, applied in two US cities, to measure 'car pride' – related to the social status and self-esteem associated with driving a car. This was found to be positively predictive of car ownership, but not the reverse. The survey was extended to 51 countries via telephone interviews, finding a wide range of scores: developed countries ranked lower than developing countries, the US having the highest score for a developed country and Japan the lowest. India and Kenya were the highest ranking of the developing economies (MIT 2019). Moody et al. (2021) estimated the value of car ownership in four US metropolitan areas by means of stated choice experiments, finding that the total value was at least as much as estimates of the average cost of private ownership, and that more than half this value was non-use value, beyond the use value of making a trip.

It is also relevant that cars are generally parked for 95 per cent of the time, which is an argument for the economic benefits of car sharing by making fuller use of a costly capital investment. Conversely, this also indicates the value of the car to individual owners, both for ready use when required, including at short notice, and also for the non-use benefits of ownership. Another indication of the non-use attractions of the car is the growth of sales of sports utility vehicles (SUVs), larger, heavier and more costly than the vehicles they replaced. In 2021, SUVs were expected to account for more than 45 per cent of global car sales (International Energy Agency 2021). While there may be some practical advantages, it seems likely that this growth reflects positive feelings about ownership of these vehicles.

While the literature on the attractions of car ownership beyond utility in use is diverse and generally persuasive, it does not offer clear indications to action to reduce car dependence. Accordingly, mitigation of the detrimental consequences of high levels of car ownership and use requires consideration of each aspect, discussed next.

1.4 Detrimental consequences of car use

The detrimental consequences of widespread car use can be tackled by improved technologies and by changing travel behaviours. This section briefly outlines the main detriments and indicates possible mitigations, the more important of which will be treated later in this book (for a fuller discussion see Metz 2022a, Chapter 1).

The most evident disadvantage of widespread car use is road traffic congestion, which arises mainly in areas with high population density where car ownership is also high. There is insufficient road capacity to accommodate all the car trips that might be made, and roads become congested. However, time is a limiting factor for travel behaviour, and some potential car users are deterred by the prospect of delays, so make other choices – to travel at a less busy time or on a less congested route, to take a different mode of travel where that is possible, to choose an alternative destination (for shopping, for instance) or not to make the trip at all (shopping online, for example).

Increasing road capacity initially relieves congestion, but that attracts previously deterred road users. Congestion is therefore substantially self-regulating, as will be discussed later (section 4.8).

The most effective means of countering road traffic congestion is by providing alternative modes of travel, particularly rail-based in all its forms, which are fast and reliable compared with cars on congested roads. The costs of rail investment can be justified mainly within and between cities, where passenger flows are substantial. Crowding on rail routes at times of peak usage is the analogue of road traffic congestion. More capacity may be made available through investment in new track and longer trains, but also in digital signalling and control technologies that enable more trains to use existing routes safely. Travel behaviour is also managed by varying fares, highest at peak times, lower at off-peak. Airlines also flex fares to manage demand in a service where crowding beyond seat capacity is not permitted.

Road traffic congestion is inconvenient and has an economic cost, but is not otherwise harmful. The most direct harmful consequence of widespread car use is poor urban air quality arising from emissions of oxides of nitrogen and of particulate matter, largely from diesel engines. These pollutants are risk factors particularly for cardiovascular and respiratory conditions, and are also associated with a variety of other disorders. Improvements to the technology of internal combustion engines and to testing regimes have substantially reduced the impact of tailpipe emissions harmful for health. Further reductions are being effected by urban traffic management schemes that limit use of the most polluting vehicles in central areas. The deployment of electric propulsion for road vehicles should make such schemes unnecessary over time. Particulates released from the wear of tyres, brakes and road surfaces have achieved greater prominence as tailpipe emissions have reduced, leading to a focus on better technologies to measure and reduce these frictional sources (Ricardo 2023).

Carbon dioxide is the other important tailpipe emission from internal combustion engines burning oil-based fuels. The consequences for climate change and the means to mitigate will be discussed in Chapter 6.

The health consequences of air pollutants are generally subtle, whereas the impact of collisions involving vehicles, their passengers and other road users may be acute, leading to deaths and serious injuries. In Britain, some 1,750 people are killed each year on the roads, and more than 25,000 are seriously injured. New roads are generally safer than historic routes, and the economic case for investment in new capacity takes account of the benefits from casualty reduction. However, schemes to convert the hard shoulder of many English motorways to running lanes, as a mean to increase capacity, led to public resistance on account of a perceived increase in danger on the event of vehicle breakdown, to which the UK government responded by cancelling new schemes. Yet the substantial level of casualties on the road network as a whole does not prompt public outcry, partly on account of habituation to this scale of carnage, which is in fact relatively low by international standards, and partly because deaths mostly occur singly and rarely to those we know (multiple fatalities, whether on the roads, railways or in the air, attract much more concern). Nevertheless, progressive authorities may adopt 'Vision Zero', the principle that it can never be ethically acceptable that people are killed or seriously injured while moving within the transport system.

One problematic feature of widespread car use is the conflicts that arise between vehicle drivers and other road users, pedestrians and cyclists, although most people will play two or all three of these roles at different times. To minimise casualties, segregation has been adopted, for instance by excluding cyclists from motorways and by creating cycle lanes in urban areas, as well as by 20 mph urban speed limits. On the other hand, segregating pedestrians from traffic by means of physical barriers is nowadays seen as detrimental to the sense of place that makes a town or city centre attractive. More generally, city streets have dual functions: to permit movement and as places for social and economic engagement. Local decisions determine the function of particular roads and the acceptability of through traffic in particular neighbourhoods. Tools to implement such decisions include limiting kerbside parking and designating Low Traffic Neighbourhoods that deter through traffic.

1.5 Air travel

The main feature of contemporary travel is the prevalence of the car, mainly for local travel but also for longer domestic journeys. But for international travel, aviation is the dominant mode. Almost 300 million passengers passed through UK airports in 2019, of which most were on leisure trips. At London's Heathrow, the largest UK airport, only 25 per cent were travelling on business, compared to 35 per cent on holiday and 37 per cent visiting relatives or friends (Department for Transport aviation statistics table AV10108). However, while 8 per cent of the population made four or more trips by air, 48 per cent made none (NTS 2019, table 0316). These 'infrequent flyers', of interest as a potential source of future demand growth, are influenced more by budget constraints and personal circumstances than specific aviation factors such as anxieties about safety or security (Graham and Metz 2017).

1.6 Inequalities

Concern about inequalities in society has increased in recent years, particularly since the 2008 financial crisis. Inequality manifests as widening ranges of income and wealth which enable the better off to gain access to superior housing and services of all kinds. The relationship between car ownership and income was noted in section 1.2. Nevertheless, transport is a relatively egalitarian domain in that there is limited scope for travelling faster by paying more. Travelling first class on trains and planes offers more comfort but no more speed, as do top-of-the-range cars in congested traffic (although road user charging could change this, see section 6.2.3).

The concept of 'transport poverty' has been conceived to describe a situation where households have to spend a large share of their money and time to meet their essential transport needs, such as travelling for work, education, healthcare, groceries and similar vital trips (Mejía Dorantes and Murauskaite-Bull 2022). In rural areas of Britain, transport accounts for the largest share of weekly household expenditure after housing costs (Salutin 2023). A related concept is 'transport-related social exclusion', meaning being unable to access opportunities, key services and community life as much as needed, and facing major obstacles in everyday life through the wider impacts of having difficulty in travelling to access key destinations. This is caused by the combination of fragmentation, unreliability and high costs in the public transport system; poor conditions for walking and cycling, in car-dominated environments; and high levels of car dependency that result – all leading to poor access to key destinations for those primarily dependent on public transport and active travel, alongside forced car ownership, in which households are compelled to have access to a car, despite the costs of car access causing them significant hardship (Transport for the North 2022).

These concepts have motivated transport researchers to address possible mitigating actions, of which improved local public transport is the main remedy. However, transport poverty is largely a consequence of income poverty, for which different societies have developed a range of remedial approaches, commonly including free-at-the-point-of-use health services and school education, funded from taxation and aimed at meeting the needs of the whole population. Subsidised travel is generally more selective. In Britain, older people may travel without charge on local public transport, as do young people in education; and people with disabilities may get public funding to access a suitable form of mechanised mobility. Local authorities may subsidise public transport routes that are not commercially viable, although subsidy is constrained by the resources available. However, subsidies benefit those users who could afford to pay the full costs, as well as those who could not. An evaluation of the scheme for free off-peak bus travel for older and disabled people in England funded by government found a benefit–cost ratio of only just over one, indicating low value for money (DfT 2016a).

There can be conflict between policies related to income inequalities and other policy objectives, particularly environmental. Tax on petrol and diesel fuels in Britain has not increased for a decade, reflecting the unpopularity of such increases, particularly for low-income motorists, even though there is a strong case for higher rates of tax to encourage the adoption of more fuel-efficient vehicles.

1.7 Conclusion

This chapter has outlined the pattern of travel behaviour in Britain prior to the coronavirus pandemic. The position of other developed economies is broadly similar. The car is the predominant mode of travel for the majority of the population who can afford the costs of ownership and who can take advantage of the speed and convenience it offers. Yet high levels of car use come with disadvantages, some of which can be mitigated through better technology and regulation. In the next chapter, we consider how we reached the present position and what past trends may imply for the future.

2
Travel trends over time

2.1 Introduction

The previous chapter outlined the main features of travel behaviour in Britain in 2019, prior to the coronavirus pandemic that caused a major shock to the transport system, as will be discussed in the following chapter. We noted the substantial reliance on the car as a common feature of travel in Britain and in all high-income economies. In this chapter, we consider how the demand for travel grew and how the transport system developed to reach the present situation, with a view to identifying the determinants of future travel demand.

2.2 Survey findings

The main features of the British National Travel Survey (NTS) were outlined in the previous chapter (section 1.2). This survey was first administered 50 years ago, so an exceptionally long time series is available, albeit with some methodological changes over the period, which nevertheless do not affect the high-level trend analysis considered here. The survey covers all modes of travel except international travel by air, and thus largely reflects daily travel behaviour. Figure 2.1 shows how three key parameters developed over this period (NTS 2019, table 0101).

The trip rate has remained steady over the period at around 1,000 trips per person per year on average. There has been some small decline in annual trips in recent years – by 9 per cent between 2002 and 2017, almost all of which was due to a reduction in walking trips of less than one mile, mainly for shopping, personal business and visiting friends (Mitchell 2018).

Figure 2.1 also shows that average travel time has remained relatively invariant at about 370 hours per person per year, close to an hour a day. In contrast, the average distance travelled by all surface modes increased

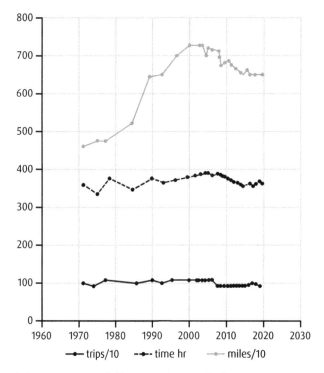

Figure 2.1 Average travel distance, time and trips per person per year in Britain. Source: National Travel Survey, table 0101.

from 4,500 miles per person per year in the early 1970s to reach 7,000 miles at the beginning of the new century, at which time growth ceased, a clear break in trend. Indeed, average distance travelled per capita fell back to about 6,500 miles in the second decade of the century.

As noted earlier, the car is the predominant mode of travel, responsible for 77 per cent of the average per capita distance travelled in 2019, a share that changed little over the previous two decades (NTS 2019, table 0409). Absolute levels of car use, driver and passenger together, declined somewhat, from 5,800 miles on average in 2002, to 5,000 miles per person per year in 2019 (NTS 2019, table 0303). This cessation of growth of per capita car travel has also been seen in many developed economies since the turn of the century (Metz 2021c). This phenomenon had originally been termed 'Peak Car', by analogy with 'Peak Oil', which refers to the expected peaking and decline in output of this finite resource (Goodwin and Van Dender 2013). However, for car use the evidence points to a cessation of growth as the prime effect, with possible long-term decline not yet generally apparent; accordingly, the term 'Plateau Car' has been proposed to designate the phenomenon (Metz 2013b).

Thus, a granular study of car ownership in England and Wales by Lower Super Output Areas (small statistical neighbourhoods designed for the census by the Office for National Statistics to have a population between 1,500 and 3,000) found that only 0.6 per cent showed a decline in cars per person between 2002 and 2018, these being areas that were primarily urban and cosmopolitan (Morgan et al. 2022).

So the two notable features of this high-level 50-year view are invariance of average travel time (and trip rate), and a marked break in trend of growth of average distance travelled.

2.3 Invariance of travel time

The available evidence indicates that long-run invariance of travel time is a general phenomenon (summarised by Metz 2021a). National travel surveys carried out in the US, Sweden, Denmark, the Netherlands and New Zealand, as well as data for individual cities with a wide range of spatial and income characteristics, are consistent with the proposition that average travel time of about an hour a day is a general feature of settled populations, with no consistent trend for this parameter to increase or decrease over the years, and with no evidence of variation with average income. This reflects the constraints imposed by the 24 hours of the day and the many activities that have to be fitted in, and the need to gain access to people, places, services and activities beyond the home for the benefits thereby available. There is, however, some variation in travel time according to age, income and regional location, as noted in the previous chapter (see section 1.2).

The implications of travel time invariance for transport investment analysis will be a focus of Chapter 4. Here we consider the growth of distance travelled, and the cessation of that growth. The key considerations are past technological innovations, contrasted with current and future innovations; demand saturation; and demographic change.

2.4 Four eras of innovation

There have been four eras of human travel, distinguished by technological developments. Modern humans emerged out of Africa some 60,000 years ago to populate the whole of the habitable Earth on foot, as hunter-gatherers.

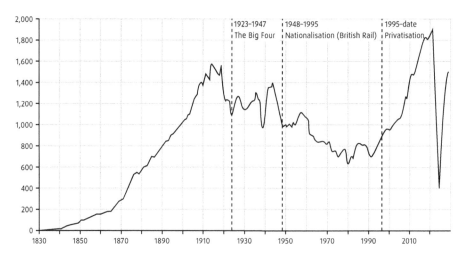

Figure 2.2 Rail passenger numbers in Britain 1830–2021. Source: Wikipedia. https://commons.wikimedia.org/wiki/File:GBR_rail_passengers_by_year_1830-2015.png.

Anthropological studies of existing such societies indicate that the time spent appropriating and preparing food may be around four or five hours a day, as influentially proposed by Sahlins (1972, 15). This implies being on the move for perhaps three or four hours a day, covering around 3,000 to 4,000 miles a year, on foot. This was the first era of travel.

When humans settled into agricultural communities, more time could be spent productively on work, limiting time for travel. Marchetti (1994) noted that the size of the territory around centuries-old Greek villages and of ancient cities was consistent with an average travel time of an hour a day. Data from contemporary low-income countries where walking predominates is consistent with the proposition that average travel time of an hour a day applies generally to settled human populations, irrespective of the state of technological development (Schafer and Victor, 2000). So in this second era of human travel, the hour-a-day time constraint limited the distance that could be travelled on foot to about 1,000 miles a year. Travel for the few who could afford horse-drawn carriages and coaches was not much faster than on foot on generally poor roads.

The third era of travel began in 1830 with the opening of the first steam-powered passenger railway between Liverpool and Manchester. This started a worldwide boom in railway construction that effected a step-change increase in the speed of travel by harnessing the energy of coal, transforming the landscape by making places accessible that had scarcely been possible hitherto. In the twentieth century, the energy of oil allowed the development and deployment of the internal combustion engine for road vehicle propulsion, and of jet engines for aircraft, again allowing step changes in speed and access. Figure 2.2 shows the rise of the railways in the nineteenth century, followed by decline in the twentieth as the car came to dominate, with a rise in the twenty-first century, the consequence of congestion on the roads, a shift of the economy from manufacturing to services, attracted to city centres by agglomeration benefits, and by investment in new trains and renovated infrastructure. At the very end of the period shown in the figure, the impact of the coronavirus pandemic can be seen, to be discussed further in the next chapter.

In the latter part of the nineteenth century, the manufacture of the modern bicycle by means of fossil fuel-powered technologies allowed human power to be used to travel faster than walking pace for local journeys, thus increasing local access beyond the home village or neighbourhood. The 1,000 miles per person per year travelled before the advent of the railways increased to some 7,000 miles in Britain by the end of the twentieth century. In other developed countries the plateau level varied according to geography, being highest in the US, where the availability of land allowed cities to sprawl.

Yet by the end of the twentieth century, the growth of per capita distance travelled powered by the energy of fossil fuels had run out of steam. The scope for increasing the speed of travel on roads by means of existing technologies is limited by the intractable nature of road traffic congestion (to be discussed in section 4.8), as well as safety concerns that are prompting reduction in speed limits, particularly in residential areas. Electric bicycles allow faster travel than conventional bicycles, yet because cycling accounts for only around 1 per cent of personal vehicle kilometres in Britain, the effect of growth of e-bikes on average distance travelled would be small. Rail travel speeds can be increased incrementally by improved track, signalling and rolling stock, and more substantially by 'high-speed rail'; the case of High Speed 2 (HS2) will be discussed later (in section 4.16.1). But again, rail accounts for a minority of personal travel trips and distance, and HS2 would be responsible for a minority of a minority, so no significant impact is to be expected on the average speed or distance travelled. In the air, the speed of travel of passenger aircraft has barely increased since the Boeing 707 first took to the air in the 1950s, although improvements to engine performance and airframe construction have increased the range between refuelling stops, which has allowed effectively faster travel over the longest routes.

The transport technology innovations of the last two centuries changed the nature of society in beneficial ways, but at a cost, as outlined in the previous chapter, of which the contribution to climate change is the most challenging. There are many new transport technologies that are now being deployed or developed, of which four are the most significant, the main features of which are outlined briefly next, with further discussion later (see also Metz 2019).

The most important innovation is electric propulsion for road vehicles using batteries to store energy. A transformational shift in engine, energy distribution and storage technologies is well underway, which will eventually eliminate tailpipe carbon and pollutant emissions, a major environmental benefit. But electric propulsion will not change the speed of travel and so will not change the access benefits of road vehicles.

There are considerable ongoing efforts to develop automated vehicle technologies, with the aspiration to deploy fully autonomous, driverless vehicles on the road network. Thus far, the scope for dispensing with human oversight seems limited, particularly in urban areas with limited road capacity and much traffic, both moving and kerbside vehicles. In theory, driverless vehicles might permit longer trips to be made since the in-vehicle time could be used for other purposes, as is the case for those using chauffeur-driven cars or taxis; yet longer trips mean more traffic and hence more congestion delays that would negate the benefit. Also in theory, driverless vehicles might operate at shorter headways and on narrower lanes, thus increasing the capacity of the infrastructure, but this would only be feasible if conventional vehicles, cyclists and pedestrians were excluded, which seems an unlikely possibility. So the general deployment of automated vehicles will be driven by the willingness of owners to pay for an improved quality of journey, without any increase in speed of travel expected.

Digital platforms that facilitate virtual, as opposed to physical, markets have been a major benefit of advances in digital technologies, notably online retail. In the transport sector, ride hailing, exemplified by Uber, has made taxi services more widely and readily available. The ability to book rail and air travel tickets online is convenient, and likewise hotel reservations when travelling. There is varying location-specific experience of the impact of ride hailing on other modes of travel, whether by adding to congestion, by competing with public transport or by facilitating use of public transport by offering a 'last mile' service to or from home. Similar varying outcomes are found for other modes based on digital platforms, including rental e-bikes and e-scooters, and demand-responsive small buses. Generally, the impact of digital platforms is in niche markets and does not change the speed of travel.

Digital navigation, generally known in the road context as 'satnav', combines the use of global positioning satellites to establish location and speed of travel, digital maps with a wealth of embedded data, and algorithms that offer shortest-time routes in the light of prevailing traffic conditions. This technology is very widely used, little of which is documented. There are three main impacts on road use (Metz 2022b). First, local users may divert to take advantage of faster trips made possible by new capacity on major roads, saving time at the cost of increased fuel consumption, but pre-empting space intended for longer distance business users, the benefit for which underpins the economic case for the investment (see section 5.4.1). Second, through traffic guided by digital navigation may take advantage of minor roads that previously had been used only by those with local knowledge, resulting in environmental detriment and conflicting with policies to promote walking and cycling for which such roads are well suited. Third, the ability of digital navigation to predict estimated travel time is the best means available to mitigate the main perceived detriment of road traffic congestion, which is the uncertainty of journey duration. Overall, the impact of digital navigation for the user is to improve the quality of the journey, with some possible increase in speed, often offset by increased distance travelled – helpful but not transformative. But there are opportunities to improve the efficiency of operation of the road network, as will be discussed in the final chapter.

The fourth era of travel, which commenced around the turn of this century, is therefore characterised by new transport technologies that enhance the quality of the environment and of the journey, without increasing the speed of travel or of access to destinations that was the main benefit of the technologies of the nineteenth and twentieth centuries. This fourth era involves a cessation of per capita growth of travel because none of the new technologies allows faster travel. This is very helpful for responding to the need to halt global warming, while the adoption of electric vehicle technology is central to reducing carbon emissions from the transport sector. The fourth era of travel is therefore the era of electrification and decarbonisation, as will be discussed in Chapter 6.

Beyond the surface modes of travel, the crucial challenge is how to decarbonise aviation, where much innovation is underway, including biofuels and synthetic fuels to be used in existing aircraft types, and battery electric and hydrogen to be used in new designs. However, there are many problems, of both feasibility and economics, and the route to Net Zero for air travel is unclear at present. But whatever technology proves possible, faster speeds seem unlikely beyond niche sectors, such as electric vertical take-off and landing aircraft for short-distance urban journeys for those willing to pay a premium fare.

2.5 Travel demand saturation

The second development that has contributed to the cessation of per capita travel growth is demand saturation.

Cessation of growth of demand for a new product or service is a common feature of all markets. Demand saturation, as it is known, reflects a sufficiency of supply of a product or service in relation to the needs of consumers. A new product that offers benefits to users is taken up, initially by early adopters, with the more cautious following later. Ownership of many kinds of domestic appliances, for instance, may exceed 90 per cent of households, in which circumstances demand is largely for replacement or to meet population growth.

There is evidence that good levels of choice of many kinds of services are available to those with use of a car or decent public transport, such that travel demand saturation may be inferred. A study by the UK competition authority found that 80 per cent of the urban population of Britain had access to three or more large supermarkets, and 60 per cent to four or more, within a 15-minute drive (Metz 2010). It is plausible that access to three or four supermarkets within 15 minutes represents a level of choice such that additional travel to reach a fourth or fifth store is unlikely to be desired – in which case the demand for travel to supermarkets has effectively been saturated. This has come about as the result of growth of car ownership, construction of additional road capacity to accommodate these vehicles and investment by retail businesses in large outlets with extensive car parking, often on land made accessible on town edges by new roads, all trends that have largely played out.

UK data on access to key services by journey time indicates high proportions of potential users having access within reasonable travel times. For example, for access to family doctors (termed general practitioners, GPs), 71 per cent of users are within 15 minutes' travel time by public transport or walking, as are 96 per cent within 30 minutes, while 87 per cent are within 15 minutes by bicycle (JTS 2017, Table 0201). Similar high levels of access are found for other services, including employment, schools, food stores and town centres.

Journey time statistics can also be used to infer levels of choice of key services. For instance, the populations of a majority of English localities have access on average to five or more GPs within a 30-minute journey by public transport/walking, and almost all localities have such choice within 15 minutes by car. Comparable levels of choice are found for other such destinations (Metz 2013a).

Demand saturation is to be expected given that the purpose of travel is to gain access to desired destinations (to be further discussed in section 4.12). Access benefits are subject to diminishing returns. Consider a person living in a village poorly served by public transport and not owning a car, thus reliant on the village shop for supplies. If this person acquires a car, they might initially save time on their journey to the village shop, but will quickly realise that they can get to the supermarket located at the nearest town, to have more choice at competitive prices, within the travel time available. If a second supermarket is available, the extra choice is beneficial, and likewise for a third and further supermarkets. But the value of each additional choice diminishes – the phenomenon of diminishing returns.

In contrast, and to simplify, the amount of access to desired locations increases with the square of the speed of travel, since what is accessible is proportional to the area of a circle, the radius of which is proportional to the speed of travel. This, though, must be qualified by the density of the road network. At the upper limit, in dense urban areas, the square of the speed would be a good approximation, whereas in remote rural areas where access is by a single road, access increases proportionately to the speed of travel.

The combination of access increasing with (up to) the square of the speed of travel but being subject to diminishing returns yields a saturation function, consistent with the observational evidence discussed above, in particular the NTS findings shown in Figure 2.1.

Nevertheless, there may exist different classes of destination with different saturation characteristics. The most common class may be termed 'replicable destinations', which can be built to meet demand. Demand for travel to replicable locations may be expected to saturate, as is likely to be the case for large supermarkets with car parks, where the past trend to open new stores seems largely to have ended, although local convenience stores are still being opened. How much choice people may seek before their demand for travel has saturated would depend on the nature of the goods or services available at the destination. For standard items generally available, such as newspapers, the nearest outlet may suffice. For more specialist items and services of variable quality and cost, people may be willing to travel further to find what they want – fashion goods, for instance, where city centres with multiple outlets justify longer journeys.

A second class of destination is what might be termed 'status destinations', applying to locations the economic concept of 'positional goods', these being locations of a unique nature or special value, which are either scarce in some absolute or socially imposed way, or subject to congestion or crowding through more intense use (Hirsch 1977; Van Wee 2021a). Examples include historic sites (from stately homes to thatched cottages), waterfront properties and Premiership football stadia. Higher speeds of travel allow access to a greater number of such distinctive non-replicable locations. However, the benefits of such enhanced access are offset by increased crowding or high prices, as others with similar interests take advantage of the improved transport facilities. Hence travel demand to gain access to status destinations may be expected to saturate. The contrast between replicable and status locations can be exemplified by the comparison of schools in general (replicable) and 'good schools' (status). Parents who are keen for their children to gain access to the latter may be willing to provide car transport to locations more distant than the nearest school, but the competition for places can be intense, which limits overall travel demand on the school run.

Demand saturation also applies to business travel. Faster travel allows businesses to gain access to more markets, whether by individuals in cars or vans, or for delivery of goods. But faster travel also exposes businesses to more competition, hence diminishing returns with an ensuing tendency to demand saturation of business travel.

One important implication of travel demand saturation is that investment in transport infrastructure must be subject to diminishing returns, as travel needs are increasingly met. However, as will be discussed in Chapter 4, the orthodox approach to the economic analysis of transport investment mainly values the saving of travel time, paying no regard to the expectation of demand saturation: hence the orthodox approach justifies nugatory expenditure.

One contributing factor to travel demand saturation is the cessation of growth of household car ownership, which increased from 14 per cent of UK households owning one or more cars or vans in 1950 to reach about 75 per cent by the end of the century, after which growth ceased, in itself an example of demand saturation. However, within car-owning households, there was a subsequent modest increase in those owning two or more vehicles, from 30 per cent in 2002 to 35 per cent in 2019 (NTS 2019, table 0205); yet the impact of this growth is fairly small since the first car is used most – the average distance travelled per person per year by those living in households with one car was 5,866 miles in 2019, while for those in households with more than one car it was 8,507 miles, an increase but not a doubling, consistent with less use being made of the second car (NTS 2019, table 0701).

Although demand saturation is a recognised concept in economic and business analysis (Osenton 2004), regrettably, the specific application to travel demand is not one that has attracted attention from researchers, even though, as outlined above, there is sufficient prima facie evidence to suppose it is relevant to travel behaviour.

2.6 Demographic change

A number of demographic changes are contributing to the cessation of growth of per capita car use (Metz 2021c). Movement of populations from country to city is a long-term global trend, reinforced in recent years in developed economies by the shift from manufacturing to business services and growth of the 'knowledge economy' that prefers to locate in city centres. Agglomeration effects offer advantages to businesses located in one geographic area, benefiting from learning, sharing and matching. Firms acquire new knowledge by exchanging ideas and information, both formally and informally; they share inputs via common supply chains and infrastructure; and they benefit by matching jobs to workers from a deep pool of labour with relevant skills. Agglomeration leads to urban development and population growth at higher densities, despite the high land prices, rents, transport and other costs. This growth has increased congestion on the urban road network and so made car use less attractive, but at the same time has improved the economic viability of public transport.

The effects of agglomeration have been seen clearly in London, the population of which fell during the period after the Second World War, but subsequently increased from 6.6 million in the 1981 census to 8.8 million in 2021 and is currently projected to increase to some 10 million by 2041. Nevertheless, car traffic in London has not increased in the past decade across London as a whole, and has decreased in Central London (TfL 2022a, section 6.3), due largely to the limited capacity of the road network. Plans were proposed in the 1960s to build more roads to accommodate the expected growth in car use. An initial section of elevated motor road was constructed westwards from central London, but this was seen as damaging to the urban fabric and plans for similar new roads around central London were largely abandoned. Thus, London has essentially retained its historic road network, which has constrained the growth of traffic. Indeed, there has been a reduction in the capacity of the road network for cars as the result of reallocation of road space to bus and cycle lanes and pedestrian uses. The consequence is that the share of journeys by car has fallen, as is borne out by the mode share data, from a peak of about 50 per cent of all trips by car at around 1990, declining to 37 per cent in 2019 (TfL 2022a, section 2.5).

The decline in the share of journeys made by car in London has also been seen in other cities with attractive centres, including Paris, Berlin, Vienna and Copenhagen; on the other hand, data from US cities indicates a continuing very high level of car use (Jones 2018; Wittwer, Gericke and Hubrich 2019). There is supporting evidence of a decline in car traffic in a number of UK cities, particularly in their centres, including Manchester and Birmingham (Metz 2013b), as well as in the major Australian cities (Newman and Kenworthy 2011). This decline in the share of journeys by car had been preceded in the second half of the last century by growth as incomes and car ownership both grew. So 'peak car' in terms of mode share was reached in London around 1990, before decline set in, a consequence of successful urban growth.

A broad distinction may be made between cities with historic central areas where the street pattern limits car use and where economic dynamism and social and cultural attractions draw a growing population, such that the population density makes public transport economically viable, in contrast to more recent cities built at low density with the car in mind as the main means of mobility and where land is available for low-density growth at the periphery. This distinction is broadly between European and North American cities, although central parts of some of the latter have high density, and suburbs of most are generally of low density. The authorities of historic cities recognise that the road network cannot be expanded to accommodate more car use without damaging the urban environment; hence decisions are made to invest in public transport, particularly rail, which provides swift and reliable travel compared with cars, buses and taxis on congested roads, as well as to improve facilities for walking and cycling such that declining car use increases the attraction of the city. In the absence of an appealing downtown district, population growth may lead to continued low-density development, with no mode shift away from car use.

The growth of the economy in cities, as well as the expansion of city centre universities, has attracted young people to move to vibrant cities to study, work, visit and live. This has contributed to a significant change in travel behaviour among young people in developed economies. A comprehensive review of the research evidence and survey data noted a trend since the mid-1990s for successive cohorts of young people (ages 17–29) to own and use cars less than their predecessors (Chatterjee et al. 2018). This contrasts with the baby boomers, born from 1946 to 1964, who led a rapid, prolonged and persistent growth in car ownership and use. Factors contributing to this trend away from car use include the cost of car ownership (not least, high insurance charges for younger drivers), problems of parking in cities and on campuses, and the viability of alternatives such as bicycles, public transport, shared car use and smartphone apps to summon a taxi. However, according to Chatterjee et al., the main causes lie largely beyond the transport system and include increased participation in higher education, for which the car is not part of the lifestyle; the use of digital communications and social media; and more generally a delayed transition to what was traditionally seen as adulthood – commitment to a career, getting married, home ownership and starting a family, with stable employment a strong determinant of being a car driver.

An important question is how this shift away from car use by young people might affect the way they travel as they get older. Stokes (2013) has shown that those who start to drive later drive less when they do start; for instance, those then in their thirties in Britain, if they learnt to drive when age 17, drove 10,000 miles a year on average, while if they learnt at age 30, they were likely to drive around 6,500 miles a year. This reduced mileage seems likely to reflect greater experience of alternative modes to the car gained before learning to drive, as well as living in places where such alternatives are viable, in particular for journeys to work. Chatterjee et al. concluded that while there are many uncertainties about the travel behaviour of future cohorts of young people, as well as about how this may change as they get older, it is nevertheless hard to envisage realistic scenarios in which all these uncertainties combine to re-establish earlier levels of car use.

As well as the impact of demographic changes discussed above, there is of course the overall growth of the population to consider. Even with stable per capita travel behaviour, population growth would increase travel demand. Generally, family size in developed economies is at historic lows: in Britain, for example, the total fertility rate in 2022 was 1.49 children per woman, a consequence of the delay of parenthood until older ages (with 2.1 being needed for a stable population). The trend of population numbers therefore substantially reflects the balance between migration inflows and outflows, both difficult to forecast. The most recent population projections of the Office for National Statistics show the UK population rising from 67.0 million to 73.7 million over the next 15 years (ONS 2024).

The implications of population growth for travel demand depend on where the additional numbers are accommodated. To the extent that this in new homes built on greenfield locations, increased car use must be expected. On the other hand, accommodation in existing urban areas, whether on brownfield land, infill sites, home extensions or redevelopment at higher density, implies that demand for public transport would be more important. In Scotland, Wales and London, the administrations have responsibility for land use planning as well as for transport, so that the location of new urban dwellings can take advantage of public transport provision. However, for England as a whole such joined-up thinking is not required, so that investment in housing and in public transport tend to be considered separately, which makes it difficult to forecast growth and mode of travel demand from projections of population growth.

2.7 Public transport trends

The corollary of the growth of car use in the second half of the last century was the decline in use of public transport, as shown in Figure 2.3. The decline and revival of rail passenger numbers has been noted earlier (Figure 2.2). Bus travel in Britain declined from 8,640 million passenger journeys a year in 1970, of which 1,500 million (17 per cent of the total) were in London, to 4,780 million in 2018/19, of which 2,200 million (46 per cent) were in London (TSGB tables BUS01 and BUS0106a). The fall in bus usage has thus been the long-term trend outside London, attributed to a shrinkage of the proportion of the population who are bus users, rather than existing bus users using the bus less often (Le Vine and White 2020). Within London, bus use reached peak usage in 2013/14 at 2,380 million passenger journeys a year, followed by a subsequent decline. On the other hand, rail use in London continued to grow until the start of the pandemic. A contributory factor to the difference between London and the rest of Britain in respect of bus usage has been the different arrangement for ownership and governance, as will be discussed below (see section 4.19).

Manville et al. (2023) have documented the pre-pandemic decline in transit ridership in Southern California ('transit' is the US term for bus and rail travel), reporting a strong association between rising private vehicle access, particularly among the populations most likely to ride transit, and falling transit use, a situation found in most other US cities.

Although air travel is not normally viewed as 'public transport', it is available to the public at large and so is not fundamentally different from rail travel, the two modes being in competition over short to medium

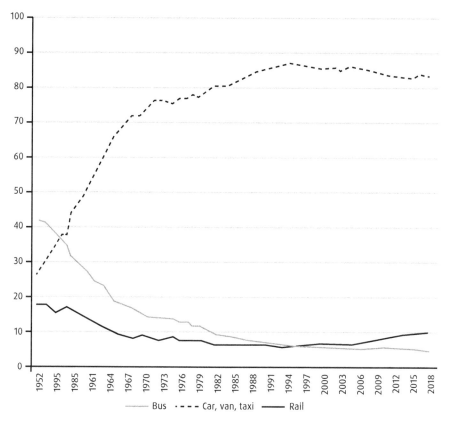

Figure 2.3 Percentage share of travel by car, trains and buses in Britain (passenger-kilometres). Source: Transport Statistics GB, table 0101.

distances. Air travel continues to grow, from 44 million passengers a year through UK airports in the mid-1970s to almost 300 million in 2019 prior to the coronavirus pandemic, with a dip following the financial crisis of 2008. The situation following the pandemic will be discussed in the next chapter.

2.8 Conclusions

There was a steady growth in per capita distance travelled as economies developed after the coming of the railways in the first half of the nineteenth century, with the car becoming the dominant mode in the course of the twentieth century. There followed a break in trend as we entered the twenty-first century, reflecting a transition from the era of fossil fuel-driven growth to that of sufficiency of travel to meet our needs.

In contrast to the growth of average distance travelled, the available evidence is consistent with long-term broadly invariant average travel time. Thus the increased speed of travel made possible by harnessing the energy of fossil fuels has been utilised to gain access to more desired destinations – people, places, activities and services, and the ensuing greater opportunities and choices – within the time constraint imposed by the 24 hours of the day and the other activities that must be fitted in.

Growth of per capita travel came to an end at the end of the last century because the existing transport technologies no longer made possible still higher speeds, while new technologies offered improvements to the quality of the journey as well as lessening environmental impact, yet without permitting faster travel. So the end of the era of travel growth was reached, which has been helpful at a time when the need to decarbonise the transport system has been recognised as a central concern.

In the twentieth century, increasing prosperity was associated with increasing car ownership and use in developed economies. In the twenty-first century, in contrast, increasing prosperity is associated with decreasing car use in big cities that have attractive centres and growing populations and that can afford to invest in an extensive network of high-quality public transport as an alternative to the car on congested roads. A question for smaller cities and towns is whether they want to follow the example of larger cities by discouraging car use to improve the urban environment and enhance economic and social interactions, to which end they would need to find resources to improve the public transport system. And a question for low-income countries, where car ownership is still relatively low, is whether the peaking of car mode share in densely populated cities can be avoided, transitioning directly to the smaller share emerging in the cities of developed economies; or whether the attractions of car ownership, discussed in section 1.3.2, make this infeasible.

A further question is whether there is scope for reducing the amount of travel, to help reduce carbon emissions. The experience of the coronavirus pandemic showed that less travel was possible, facilitated by information technology developments that permitted remote working and meetings, as will be discussed in the next chapter.

3
Shock of the pandemic

3.1 Introduction

The coronavirus pandemic caused major dislocation in society, not least to the amount and modes of travel, with many similarities across countries, albeit differing in detail depending on constraints imposed on work and travel (ITF 2023). This amounted to a 'natural experiment' in that an exogenous event led to large changes in travel behaviour over a two-year period, before the cause faded away and normal life resumed, yet with some likely permanent long-term consequences.

The general course of the pandemic and the public health interventions adopted in response are well known. Figure 3.1 shows the changing pattern of travel in London, not dissimilar to that found elsewhere in Britain, with patterns in other countries reflecting local experiences and decisions. Overall travel behaviour responded to policy interventions, principally 'lockdowns' that prohibited movement and social mixing of various categories of persons. As these were removed, car use bounced back the most rapidly, reflecting the security from airborne infection offered by the private car. Public transport use returned much more slowly.

The pandemic led to two main changes in how we lived and in the related demand for travel: more working from home and more shopping online.

3.2 Working from home

While some who did not need face-to-face contact with customers, clients or colleagues have always worked from home, the pandemic resulted in a step change in the numbers adopting this mode. In some cases, this was a suboptimal response to an emergency, for instance in the education sector. In other cases, this reflected some advantages of not travelling to

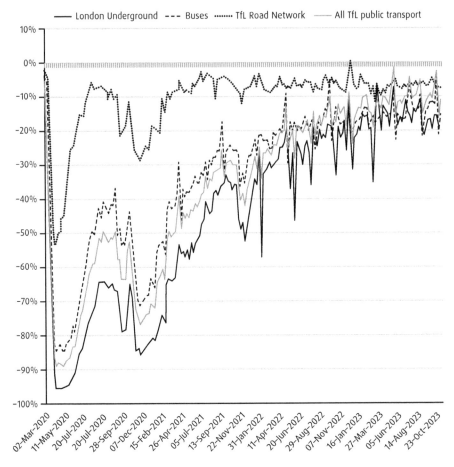

Figure 3.1 Average weekly demand on London's transport networks compared to the equivalent week before the pandemic. Source: Transport for London, Travel in London Report 15.

a workplace for at least part of the week: avoiding both the time and the discomfort of commuting, flexibility of when to work and perhaps the avoidance of interruptions in the privacy of the home environment.

For some organisations, it has been found that the workplace office could be dispensed with entirely. For many others, some form of hybrid working has emerged, with employees spending part of the week in the office, although the long-term stability of this outcome is yet to be seen. The extent of hybrid working reflects a balance between the preference of many employees for working at home and the preference of many of their managers for having people in the office – for oversight, to stimulate creative interactions and to induct new staff into the culture and practices of the organisation. This balance is affected by the state of the employment market – the demand and supply of employees with appropriate skills. The market was tight following the pandemic, with low levels of unemployment as many older workers decided not to return. But over time, this balance could shift, particularly if the benefits of agglomeration in particular sectors are as significant as had previously been supposed, so that businesses that have more staff on site prove to be more successful and profitable. On the other hand, businesses that commit to hybrid working may be able to attract employees from a wider area, as well as reducing the expense of maintaining office space for the full complement of staff.

Surveys of working adults in Britain found that while 50 per cent reported working from home at some point in the previous seven days in the first half of 2020, early in the pandemic, this had fallen to 40 per cent in early 2023; throughout 2022, when the restrictions of the pandemic had been lifted, the percentage of working adults reporting having worked from home varied between 25 and 40 per cent, without a clear upward or downward trend, indicating that home working is resilient to the end of travel restrictions (ONS 2023a). Professionals and those in higher income bands were more likely to work from home, whereas those who require face-to-face contact with clients or personal engagement with materials resumed travelling to their workplace – in education, healthcare, hospitality, retail, manufacturing and laboratories.

A survey of central London workers in April 2023 found that they came into the office on average for 2.3 days a week, 59 per cent of pre-pandemic levels; of those going into work, the most popular hybrid model was two days in the workplace – 30 per cent of workers did so, while almost half of workers went into their workplace for at least three days, with Tuesdays and Wednesdays the most common days in the office, and Friday the least popular (Swinney et al. 2023).

US data shows that 60 per cent of days were worked from home early in the pandemic, declining and stabilising to around 30 per cent after early 2022, reflecting an apparent permanent increase in working from home. By the first half of 2023, 15 per cent of full-time employees were fully remote, 56 per cent were full-time in the workplace and 29 per cent were in a hybrid arrangement. However, there was a difference of about half a day between worker desire to work from home and (higher) employer wishes. A wide range of working from home rates was found according to industry, ranging from 2.55 days per week for the information sector to 0.65 for hospitality and food (Barrero, Bloom and Davis 2023).

Surveys of employees in 34 countries found higher levels of working from home in English-speaking countries. Full-time employees worked from home 1.4 days a week in the United States as of March–April 2023, more than any other country except Canada (1.7 days) and the United Kingdom (1.5 days). By way of comparison, the average across 15 countries in continental Europe was only 0.8 days a week, with a maximum of 1.0 days in Germany and the Netherlands. The average across six Asian countries (China, Malaysia, Japan, Singapore, South Korea and Taiwan) was 0.7 days a week (Aksoy et al. 2023).

Barrero, Bloom and Davis (2023) have discussed the factors contributing to high levels of working from home as this varies across countries, including size of residence and scope for accommodating a home office, a high share of employment in the business services sector, the ability of managers to evaluate staff performance remotely and favourable experience of managing the pandemic, lessening the need to work from home.

The emergence of a 'new normal' involving fully remote and hybrid working raises a question about the value of agglomeration benefits from learning, sharing and matching in city centres (see section 2.6). Estimation of the economic value of agglomeration has been based on econometric analysis addressing the change in productivity in relation to the change in effective economic density, with the biggest benefits accruing to knowledge-focused businesses, despite remote or hybrid working being most feasible for such businesses. However, the observed movement of businesses to central locations in recent decades reflects net agglomeration benefits, the positive benefits being offset by the negative, and the balance being affected by technological developments.

Fleet Street, for instance, was once the physical location of the national newspapers in central London, with printing presses in the basements, print workers on floors above and editorial staff on the upper floors. This was a classic cluster, with benefits from shared facilities and staff, allowing news to travel faster and gossip to flourish. But there were offsetting disbenefits: newsprint had to be brought into central London, from where newspapers were distributed across the country overnight, and there were restrictive labour practices reflecting trade union power when the product had to be made anew each day. However, the advent of digital typesetting allowed newspapers to be printed at remote printworks with better access to transport networks, so that the editorial offices could disperse to scattered locations around London. Nowadays, 'Fleet Steet' is a metaphor for the newspaper industry, no longer the actual location. With hindsight, the agglomeration benefits and disbenefits were more finely balanced than had been supposed, so that new technology could tilt the balance in favour of dispersion of the cluster.

A question, then, is whether something similar may be happening more generally to knowledge-based businesses that had been benefiting from clustering in city centres. It has long been suggested that modern information and telecommunications would lead to the 'death of distance' (Cairncross 1997), yet the benefits of agglomeration seemed to trump those associated with dispersal. But then the shock of the pandemic both enforced working from home where possible and brought forward technologies to facilitate online meetings and collaboration based on broadband telecommunications that had steadily been improving. The disbenefits of agglomeration to employees in the form of the time, cost and discomfort of commuting became immediately apparent, with a consequential reluctance to return full-time to the workplace. It is therefore possible that the balance of benefits and disbenefits may have shifted in favour of dispersal. On the other hand, in some sectors the benefits of staff attending the workplace are being recognised: the head of the UK government's Infrastructure and Projects Authority has observed a 9–12 month extension of design duration as a result of hybrid working, leading to higher costs and delayed completion (Smallwood 2023). Thus it may take time for working practices to reach a settled outcome.

For employers, increased working from home could lead to a decrease in demand for office space in the centres of cities, although this would depend on how workspace is managed to accommodate staff who are there for only part of the week. Shrinkage of space to save rental costs could make the office a less attractive destination. High-quality premises with good facilities within and nearby would be preferred, to attract high-quality staff. Older, lower-quality buildings are becoming redundant, particularly on account of regulatory requirements to improve the energy efficiency of rented buildings. This presents opportunities to repurpose such redundant workplaces, as has long been the case by creating loft apartments from historic warehouses. The scope for repurposing more recent office accommodation can be limited by the depth of floorplan, since windows would be expected by residents of flats, and by the core location of services. Creation of laboratory space, hotels and student accommodation is being considered. Perhaps the simplest repurposing would be a reversion to residential use of inner-city eighteenth- and nineteenth-century houses built for families with servants but subsequently converted to offices. Such repurposing would fit the concept of the 15-minute city or 20-minute neighbourhood where most needs can be met by active travel within a short distance. However, with many tenants and landlords bound by long-term leases, it will take time for the full extent of the changes to occupancy to emerge.

While reduced use of public transport for commuting means less crowding at peak times, it also results in less revenue for the operators and so either more subsidy is required, or the outcome is poorer service and/or higher fares. This raises the question of the role of bus and rail travel in sustaining the economic and social vibrancy of towns and cities, particularly those whose density is such the general use of the car is not viable. The scope for raising fares is limited by the use made by those who cannot afford a car, which means that some external source of funding support is required. Support from government was increased substantially during the pandemic as an emergency measure, but the longer-term position remains to be seen. Transport for London (TfL) has been more dependent on operating income from passenger revenue than other major cities: London 72 per cent, New York 38 per cent, Paris 38 per cent, Madrid 47 per cent, Hong Kong 37 per cent, Singapore 21 per cent (TfL 2021b, 5.8.43). Hence TfL was hit harder by the loss of fare income during the pandemic so that tortuous negotiations with central government were required to avoid serious loss of services. The case for increased external subsidy to sustain high-quality public transport fits well with the need to decarbonise the transport sector by offering alternatives to car use, given that internal-combustion engine vehicles will be dominant for some years to come. Another source of subsidy could be from road pricing for electric vehicles, as will be discussed later (section 6.2.3).

It is possible that the time saved by commuting less will be used for other travel, given the long-run invariant hour a day of travel time. If this other travel is local active travel, cycling or walking, that would be helpful for reducing the environmental impact; if by car, less so, particularly if commuting had been by public transport. Working from home also allows living more remotely from the workplace if travel to work is less frequent; this leads to changes in residential property prices between urban and rural locations, and new construction where land with planning consent is available for development, with consequential changes for travel behaviour, particularly increased car use.

An analysis based on the American Time Use Survey investigated how commuting time saved during the pandemic was used: total working time was reduced while leisure time and sleeping increased, findings consistent with employees' preferences for working from home, although whether increased leisure activity was within or beyond the home was not indicated (Dam et al. 2022). On the other hand, UK time use data

indicated that less time was spent sleeping but more time outside, whether travelling, socialising or shopping, between the first lockdown in March 2020 and a year later (ONS 2021).

3.3 Online shopping

The other shift prompted by the pandemic was to online retail, growth of which was accentuated markedly. Yet shopping is also a social activity, and the suitability of many goods is best judged first hand, whether the feel and look of fashion items or the bulk of furnishings. Data for internet sales as a proportion of total retail sales had been on a steadily increasing trend before the pandemic, rising from around 3 per cent in 2007 to 19 per cent immediately before the pandemic (paralleled by a decline in shopping trips: NTS 2019, table 0403). It spiked to reach 38 per cent in early 2021 before falling back to 25 per cent in mid-2022, broadly returning to trend (ONS 2023b). Linear growth cannot continue indefinitely, of course, but the timing of declining growth and plateau cannot be forecast as yet.

The main impact of this shift to online shopping has been to reduce the attractiveness of city centre department stores, some chains of which have closed entirely while others have shut some branches and repurposed upper-floor space in continuing locations. Stronger city centres that relied on a wide catchment area were most affected by the pandemic, while high streets in economically weaker cities and towns were less affected, although many were already experiencing difficulty in attracting shoppers and shops on account both of general economic conditions in towns that had lost major industries and the shift to online retail (Centre for Cities 2022). Over time, rents will adjust to a lower demand for retail floor space, allowing either new entrants or repurposing for other uses.

3.4 Travel demand post-pandemic

By April 2022, motor vehicle use in Britain had returned to just over 100 per cent of pre-pandemic levels (DfT 2023e). Public transport use grew back at slower rates and some components have tended to remain below pre-pandemic levels: by late 2023, national rail use was around 85 per cent of that observed in the same period in 2019. London Underground use was a little higher, and bus use was about 90 per cent, although there have been significant fluctuations due to school holidays, weather events, tourist flows and industrial action.

Data published by Transport for London provide a more granular account of the position as of late 2023 (see Figure 3.1). Overall public transport demand reached 90 per cent of the pre-pandemic baseline while cycling in 2022 was responsible for 4.5 per cent of trips, up from 3.6 per cent in 2019. There has been a consolidation of weekday travel on Tuesdays to Thursdays, where demand is typically higher than on Mondays and Fridays (particularly on rail modes), although only 26 per cent of all London residents have the option to work from home, reflecting a 'blue collar' versus 'white collar' difference. There is also more travel on weekends than on some weekdays, and slightly longer average journey lengths, all of which appear to be becoming established features of post-pandemic demand (TfL 2023).

There is further evidence of variation in return to public transport according to social group. Thus, analysis of smartcard data from senior citizens in the West Midlands metropolitan region found that male, relatively younger and non-white passengers were the earliest to return to public transport while those from a white ethnic background and affluent areas were slower (Long, Carney and Kandt 2023).

There was a burst of recreational cycling during the first lockdown, reaching a peak, nationally, of 63 per cent above a 2013 baseline in mid-2021, falling back to a 24 per cent increase above 2013 in late 2022, consistent with a modest rate of long-term growth (DfT 2023f). Although there were many adaptations to urban roads at the outset of the pandemic to facilitate cycling as an alternative to crowded public transport, the ultimate impact of this will not be clear until the extent of return to the office becomes evident (see below).

The previous chapters discussed travel demand up to 2019, based largely on the National Travel Survey. Comparison of key parameters for the two years of the pandemic, 2020 and 2021, with the years immediately before and after is shown in Table 3.1. The data for 2022 as a whole show only partial return to pre-pandemic levels, which may reflect the emergence of the Omicron variant of Covid in late 2021, even though travel restrictions were lifted by February 2022. The average travel time prior to the pandemic was close to 60 minutes a day; during 2020 and 2021 it fell to about 45 minutes, but rose in 2022 to 53 minutes. It would not be surprising if average travel time returned to close to an hour a day in 2023, although it remains too early to rule out some longer-term change in travel behaviour, most likely arising from increased working from home. Thus, the average number of commuting trips in 2022 was 85 per cent of that in 2019, whereas the average number of education trips (including escorting) was 94 per cent of the

	Trips	Distance	Time
2019	953	6,500	370
2020	739	4,334	269
2021	757	4,329	273
2022	862	5,373	324

Table 3.1 Average annual number of trips, distance travelled (miles) and travel time (hours). Source: National Travel Survey 2022.

earlier year, indicating the greater opportunity for working from home in contrast to studying at home. Average car mileage in 2022 was 89 per cent of that in 2019.

A detailed survey of travel choices of adults in England in November 2022, compared with the pre-pandemic period, found significant declines in use of public transport: 48 per cent using bus versus 63 per cent pre-pandemic; 43 per cent using train (vs 63 per cent); and 29 per cent using Underground/metro (vs 44 per cent). Likewise for the proportions walking, 68 per cent (vs 79 per cent), and cycling, 26 per cent (vs 31 per cent). However, the proportions who travelled by car as driver or passenger were similar to pre-pandemic, with increased informal car-pooling at 21 per cent (vs 15 per cent) (Marshall et al. 2023). The frequency of travelling to work had fallen: 32 per cent of employed people travelled to a place of work five days a week or more often in November 2022 compared with 47 per cent immediately before the pandemic.

The NTS covers domestic travel. Air travel before the pandemic had been on a rising trend since 2011 to reach 258 million international passenger movements through UK airports in 2019 (DfT Aviation statistics table AVI 0105). The pandemic caused major disruption to air travel, reducing numbers to 50 million in 2021, but in 2022 numbers recovered to 75 per cent of 2019 levels. Leisure travel bounced back much faster than business travel, the future extent of which is still unclear, given the habit of remote working acquired during the pandemic, and the experience of operational difficulties on the part of both airlines and airports. Airlines are reportedly taking a bullish view, placing large orders for new aircraft, perhaps prompted by the recollection that international business travel has been slower to recover from past economic downturns than leisure travel.

3.5 Conclusions

A key question is whether the travel changes triggered by the pandemic will have long-term impacts that will help achieve transport decarbonisation. The evidence is that car use rebounded to pre-pandemic levels faster than public transport use, where full recovery has yet to occur, and may not do so if working from home persists as an alternative to the full week in the workplace. Active travel at best shows a slow growth trend.

The pandemic has shown that we could make major changes to lifestyle and travel behaviour under the impetus of concerns about personal health. Coming out of the pandemic, some analysts saw indications of a long-term shift to travelling less, notably those working from home making less use of the car (Anable et al. 2022). It is possible that working from home will prove to be a long-term feature for those for whom it is practicable and where employers are amenable, resulting in more agreeable and less crowded and congested commuting. Yet this leaves open whether and how the saving in commuting time might be used, whether for non-travel activities or for other kinds of journey, and by what mode.

While the full impact of the pandemic on travel behaviour is therefore not yet clear, the emerging evidence suggests we largely reverted to pre-pandemic travel behaviour, particularly by car, once the threat to health had receded. The impetus of the climate emergency is less immediately pressing, and so we persist in travel behaviour that meets our needs for access to people, places, activities and services, with the opportunities and choices that ensue, hoping that advances in technology would avoid having to make hard choices about travelling less. Those seeking substantial reductions in car use to mitigate climate change can take but little comfort from the pandemic experience.

4
Transport economics reconsidered

4.1 Introduction

Over the past half century, the sub-discipline of transport economics has developed largely in a silo outside the economics mainstream. An important application has been to the cost–benefit analysis of new investments in infrastructure and vehicles by the public sector. The main economic benefit of new investment that allows faster travel is assumed to be the saving of travel time. As a meeting of experts convened by the intergovernmental International Transport Forum concluded:

> Measuring the reduction in travel time has long been a fundamental element of the economic case for transport infrastructure investment. Reducing the amount of time spent on travel enables transport users to spend the time they have saved more productively or more enjoyably. For over fifty years, techniques have been developed and refined to put a monetary value on reduction in travel time made available by investment in transport. This value that can be measured has made it possible for policy makers to be well informed about the benefits of the project and allows them to compare the value of reductions in travel time with the costs of the project (including financial, social and environmental costs). Further, the costs and the benefits can be weighted, facilitating an evidence-based decision about the merits of the project. (ITF 2019, 9)

Considerable efforts have been expended to attribute monetary values to time savings according to mode and purpose of travel. Yet in reality, average travel time has not changed for many decades (see section 2.3), despite huge investment justified by the value of travel time savings.

To understand this apparent paradox, it is necessary to outline the main features of the orthodox approach to transport investment analysis, also termed transport investment appraisal ('appraisal' for short). There are many sources, including Jara-Diaz 2007, Nellthorp 2017 and articles in a recent compilation edited by Vickerman (2021). The UK Department for Transport issues a regularly updated Web-based compilation, Transport Analysis Guidance, intended to be a comprehensive, authoritative and accessible source covering standard approaches to transport modelling and appraisal methods that are applicable for highways and public transport interventions, references to which hereafter will take the form 'TAG [section and paragraph number],[date of publication]', for instance 'TAG A1.3, 2020', which is the section relevant to the discussion that follows, and which is based on UK practice, the development of which has been chronicled by Worsley and Mackie (2015). Practice in other countries is broadly similar, although there are some differences of values, emphasis and content (Mackie, Worsley and Eliasson 2014).

The chapter that follows, the longest in this book, is a detailed and evidenced critique of a well-established approach to the economic appraisal of transport investments, so it may be useful to signpost its content:

- Sections 4.2–3 set the scene, pointing out the inconsistency between the saving of travel time regarded as the main benefit of transport investment and the observed invariance of travel time.
- Sections 4.4–6 offer a detailed analysis of the time-saving methodology, which need not be read closely by those who are mainly concerned with the broader picture.
- Sections 4.7–8 discuss the implications of investment for traffic on the road network.
- Sections 4.9–11 consider the wider economic impacts of transport investment.
- Section 4.12 discusses the nature of access benefits.
- Sections 4.13–15 considers the implications of diversity, the impact of externalities and active travel.
- Section 4.16 provides case studies of investments in rail, road and air travel.
- Sections 4.17–18 discuss the strategic case for transport investments and related matters of governance.
- Sections 4.19–20 briefly note the economics of competition and limits of economic analysis.
- Section 4.21 presents a summary and conclusions.

4.2 Orthodox transport investment appraisal

The basic assumption is that users of the transport system perceive both money costs and time costs associated with the trips they make. When someone makes a trip, these costs will be outweighed by the opportunities and benefits at the destination. The notion of 'consumer surplus', a standard concept of microeconomics, applies here and is defined as the benefit which a consumer enjoys in excess of the costs that they perceive.

For example, if a journey would be undertaken provided it takes no more than 20 minutes, but not if it takes more than 20 minutes, then the benefit of the journey to the traveller is equivalent to a cost of 20 minutes of travel time. If actual travel time for the journey is only 15 minutes, then the traveller enjoys a surplus of 5 minutes. The benefits to users of a transport improvement that changes the perceived costs of travel are based on the change in this surplus. If such an improvement reduces the travel time in this example to 12 minutes, it would increase the traveller's surplus by 3 minutes (TAG A1.3, 2.1.2, 2022).

Time is a valuable resource, so that if the time required for a journey could be reduced, travellers would experience a benefit in that they would have more time available for other desired activities, whether at home, at work or elsewhere. In general, travel time savings are seen as the main benefit from transport infrastructure investments such as increased road capacity and improved rail routes. Estimating a monetary value for travel time savings (VTTS) allows this benefit to be included with other benefits whose monetary value can be estimated, for instance reduced deaths and injuries from collisions. Offsetting disbenefits, such as increased vehicle operating costs, are also taken into account. Small (2012) has stated that it is difficult to name a concept more widely used in transportation analysis than the value of travel time. (Daly and Hess (2020) argue that the term Value of Travel Time (VTT) is more appropriate than the widely employed Value of Travel Time Savings (VTTS), but the distinction is not central to the discussion below.)

A standard concept is the 'generalised cost' of travel, comprising time costs (in monetary terms), money costs and any other sources of disutility from travel (such as crowding on public transport). Comparison of estimates of generalised costs with and without a contemplated investment generates the overall monetary benefits of the investment. These can then be compared with the costs of investment, in conventional cost–benefit analysis using discounted cash flows over time.

An improvement to a transport route or service that reduces generalised cost is of benefit to regular users. But the cost reduction attracts additional users, for whom the cost would previously have been a deterrent to travel. In this context, conventional microeconomic analysis involves:

- estimation of demand as a function of cost (as cost declines, demand increases);
- estimation of the cost of supply as a function of demand (as demand increases, costs increase, for instance on account of delays due to traffic congestion);
- an equilibrium is established when the generalised costs that users are willing to pay for the journey equal the marginal cost of supplying it;
- at this equilibrium, it is possible to estimate the consumer surplus;
- reduction in the cost of supply arising from investment benefits regular users by increasing their consumer surplus. But there will also be new users, attracted by the lower cost, for whom it is supposed the benefit will be half that accruing the regular users. Taking both regular and new users together yields a formula, known as the 'rule-of-a-half', for estimating consumer surplus as a result of the investment.

This brief, very compressed outline of the microeconomic analysis that is the basis for conventional transport investment appraisal will be familiar to many readers. A fuller treatment is available in standard texts. There are, however, a number of fundamental problems, as discussed in the following sections, appreciation of which do not depend on a detailed exposition of the conventional approach.

4.3 Invariance of travel time

As discussed in Chapter 2, there is considerable observational data indicating that travel time, averaged across a population, is stable at around an hour a day. Such empirical, long-run stability raises questions about the assumptions implicit in orthodox transport investment appraisal and modelling (Metz 2008; Metz 2021a). The possibility of short-run travel time savings is not precluded, but in the longer run, the implication of observed travel time invariance is that potential time savings are used to travel further, taking advantage of the higher speed of travel generally made possible by investments and improvements to reach more distant destinations, achieving more access to people, places, activities and services with enhanced opportunities and choices.

The observed invariance of average travel time has prompted consideration of the notion of a 'travel time budget', implying that individuals have a certain amount of time they are willing to spend on travel and that they will minimise departures from that budget. While it has long been recognised that only a certain amount of time is available for travel within the 24-hour day, the pioneering studies of Zahavi (1974) led him to articulate the concept of a travel time budget and discuss the implications for travel behaviour.

The relevant literature has been reviewed by Mokhtarian and Chen (2004) and by Ahmed and Stopher (2014), who point out that a travel time budget is not directly observable, unlike travel time expenditure, which is measurable. The observed variation of travel time expenditure as a function of age and income implies that individuals are making choices of activities that involve the expenditure of time, just as they make choices about the expenditure of money. Daily expenditure of time is constrained by the 24 hours available to all, whereas money expenditure varies with income, which is unequally distributed and changes across the life course. As with money, there is an opportunity cost to time spent travelling, time that cannot be used for other desired activities, which sets an upper bound. On the other hand, reducing daily travel time tends to lessen access to opportunities that are spatially separated, as well as to the intrinsic benefits of mobility, which include physical movement as a human need, social participation, expression of personal autonomy, and movement as a source of stimulation and diversion (Mokhtarian, Salomon and Singer 2015).

Mental accounting of personal financial activities is a well-established subject of investigation (Thaler 1999). However, there appear to be no analogous studies of travel time budgets to be attributed to individuals. Nevertheless, the observed invariance of average travel time implies both upper and lower bounds to time that can be expended on travel, considerations that can inform our understanding of travel behaviour and are central to decisions on transport investment and policy. The past growth of average distance travelled, as discussed in Chapter 2, is necessarily the result of faster travel in unchanged travel time, a consequence of investment – very largely private investment in more and better road vehicles and public investment in roads, as recognised by Metz (2008) and Ahmed and Stopher (2014).

Faster travel allows greater access to desired destinations, to more people, places, activities and services, thus enhancing opportunities and choices. The main benefits of investment are therefore access benefits, rather than the saving of travel time that permits more productive work or valued leisure. This has become recognised by responsible authorities. As noted by the International Transport Forum (ITF 2017, 9):

> Appraisal of transport projects has traditionally focused on travel time savings and congestion relief. However, there is a growing understanding that this misses the ultimate purpose of the transport system, which is to provide access to employment, goods, services and other opportunities.

This perspective was reiterated subsequently (ITF 2022, 11):

> Transport policy and planning objectives are being fundamentally rethought in many OECD countries. A central element of this shift is the increasing move to replace the traditional mobility focus of transport planning with an accessibility-based perspective. The accessibility perspective recognises that transport is a derived demand and that the purpose of passenger transport policy is to enable people to reach destinations to participate in various activities.

The UK Department for Transport's (DfT) Integrated Rail Plan for the North and the Midlands (DfT 2021a, 39) acknowledged that:

> Over the last 50 years the time people spend travelling has remained relatively constant, though distances travelled have increased . . . Overall, people have taken the benefits of better transport links as the ability to access a wider range of jobs, business and leisure opportunities, rather than to reduce total time spent travelling.

It is noteworthy that the DfT has not seen fit to revise its Transport Analysis Guidance, to reflect this recognition of the importance of access as the long run benefit of transport investment.

Travel time savings may, nevertheless, be relevant in the short run – in particular, immediately after new road capacity becomes available. An example can clarify the distinction between short-run and longer-run benefits of investment. A person living in a village poorly served (if at all) by public transport and not owning a car is limited in their choice of shops and other services to those accessible on foot. Acquisition of a car may initially allow a few minutes of time to be saved going to the village shop, but it is soon realised that the supermarket with car park, located at the nearby town, with a greater range of goods at competitive prices, can be accessed in the time available. Similar changes in travel occur over more extended periods as individuals who have acquired cars seek new employment or move house, the benefits being more access to choices and opportunities. Private investment in cars has been complemented by public investment in roads to permit the access benefits made possible by car ownership to be realised.

Later in this chapter we will consider how access benefits might be valued, as well as the wider implications of travel time invariance. But first, we will note some problems that arise in the use of the orthodox time savings methodology that raise questions about its utility for the appraisal of transport investments.

4.4 Problems with valuing travel time savings

The economic benefit of an investment that allows faster travel is estimated as the product of three factors: the time saved per traveller, the number of travellers and the monetary value of time. Valid estimates of the value of time are therefore crucial to the economic appraisal of transport investments based on cost–benefit analysis.

When valuing time savings, it is conventional to distinguish between travel on business and non-work travel, the latter being in turn subdivided between commuting and other purposes. For business travel, it had been the practice to base the value of time savings on labour costs, on the assumption that productive work could not be carried out while travelling, while for non-work travel, a willingness-to-pay (WTP) approach has been adopted (see below). However, the advent of digital technologies allows productive work while travelling by train, which affects the value of journey time savings (Wardman and Lyons 2016; Wardman, Chintakayala and Heywood 2020).

Accordingly, the most recent research commissioned by the United Kingdom DfT, aimed at estimating updated values of time savings, extended the WTP approach to business travel, in part to address how factors such as the ability to work on a train may affect such values, on the assumption that WTP should reflect how time is used (Batley et al. 2017). The following discussion considers the problems arising from this research (Metz 2017; see also Mackie, Batley and Worsley 2018). Hess, Daly and Börjesson (2020) have also offered a critique of the DfT-commissioned research from a perspective that did not dispute the relevance of monetary values of travel time, but concluded that the research approach employed was too simplistic.

In establishing WTP values of travel time savings, respondents to what is known as a stated preference (SP) survey were asked which option for a hypothetical journey they preferred: one quicker and more expensive, the other cheaper and slower. This highlights the short-run focus of this approach, whereas the purpose of valuing travel time savings is to appraise the value for money of long-lived investments. Moreover, it was recognised that there is ambiguity around precisely to which road conditions, in terms of congestion, the resulting values of time relate; and the idea that a faster journey would be more expensive, in terms of fuel costs, is not intuitive since using a motorway could be more economical than a slower route involving stops and starts.

Three types of SP experiment were carried out (Batley et al. 2017, 588): one a straightforward trade-off between time and cost; a second with the added factor of journey time reliability, involving comparisons of trips with narrow or wide range of time outcomes; and a third in which the quality of the journey was varied by specifying the level of road traffic congestion or, for public transport, both frequency of service and crowding. However, the values of time from the reliability experiment were markedly higher than from the simple case, and the possibility was recognised that these had been influenced or biased upwards by the instructions given in the questionnaire. This illustrates the sensitivity of SP values to the precise experimental arrangement.

An effort was made to compare SP and revealed preference (RP) approaches for the same set of options for rail travel, where multiple operators offered a range of different journey times and fares, so that examination of ticket sales could indicate trade-offs between time and money. However, this was not successful since a large amount of data had to be excluded from the modelling in order that viable results could be estimated; and moreover, both RP and SP models produced very high values of time. Thus, this attempt failed to validate the hypothetical SP experiments by reference to real observed behaviour. (However, more recently, Tsoleridis, Choudhury and Hess (2022) have reported that a GPS trip diary, coupled with a background household survey, have the ability to provide VTT estimates statistically equal to national values derived from traditional SP surveys.)

The requirement for appraisal is values of time that do not depend on the point of reference of the participant in the SP experiment, who would normally be influenced by the perceived nature of the difference (gain or loss) or scale (large or small). The research found evidence of significant reference dependence in survey responses in that the estimated value of time savings was sensitive to the size of the time saving offered in the SP experiment (Batley et al. 2017, 605). The attempt was made to 'neutralise' size effects by adopting a time saving of 10 minutes for the purpose of specifying the value of time, a judgement based on a review of the relevant literature. However, this is substantially more than the average time saving of three minutes from the post-opening project evaluations of major highway schemes (Highways Agency 2011). The attempt to 'neutralise' reference dependence was therefore problematic. More generally, Ojeda-Cabral, Hess and Batley (2018) concluded that values of time vary with such settings of the variables of the SP experiments.

Quite substantial changes were found in the monetary values of time between previously determined values and those from the more recent research. For instance, time spent commuting was worth £10.01 per hour in 2010 prices, in contrast to the previous value of £6.81. It is hard to judge to what extent this reflects changes in methodology, as opposed to changes in real values. Subsequently, a study of VTTS data from the Netherlands and Sweden collected 13–14 years apart found declining values, contrary to expectation, attributed to methodological issues, including declining response rates to surveys (Börjesson et al. 2023).

Altogether, the research study of Batley et al. (2017) attempted to fit a diversity of observations into a theoretical framework, dealing with uncertainties and inconsistencies through the exercise of judgement on the part of a group of investigators committed to the overall approach and to advancing the state of the art. This struggle to achieve consistency points up the questionable basis for valuing time savings as the main benefit of transport investment.

4.5 Valuing reliability and congestion

The analysis discussed above, to derive the estimates of the value of time, employed a joint modelling approach across different SP experiments, simultaneously estimating values of time, reliability and crowding/ traffic conditions. It was also possible to estimate values for reliability, punctuality and comfort in terms of a 'multiplier' – the 'reliability ratio' – a factor by which the value of time saving is multiplied to provide a measure of the value of reliability etc. The outcome of the SP experiments involving reliability led to the proposal that the reliability ratio be reduced from the previous value of 0.8 to 0.4, so that the value attached to journey time reliability in appraisal should be halved (Batley et al. 2017, 612).

However, it is hard to justify such a major change to the value to be ascribed to reliability on the basis of a single set of SP experiments involving variations in both time and reliability. Reliability and time savings are conceptually distinct and the former could be valued in SP experiments dedicated to that purpose, which would increase confidence in the findings, particularly because reliability benefits from investment are short-run whereas notional times savings are a proxy for long-run changes affecting land use. Moreover, reducing the perceived experience of unreliability through the provision of predictive journey time information by the providers of digital navigation services need not affect travel time and so should be valued in an unrelated way. The same argument applies to crowding on the railway, the relief of which through longer or more frequent trains is unrelated to journey time.

The research of Batley et al. (2017) also found evidence that VTTS varied with the level of traffic congestion. However, multipliers to reflect this were not included in updated DfT guidance (TAG A.1.3, 2017) because they appeared very high – some three-fold, comparing heavy congestion with free flow conditions (Batley, Dekker and Mackie 2022). This implies that car travellers would be willing to travel significantly longer distances to avoid heavy traffic, for which there is indeed evidence (see section 5.4.1). This willingness to travel further presumably reflects drivers' preference to keep moving, rather than be stuck in congested traffic. However, were the VTTS of employees travelling on employers' business to be based on labour costs as heretofore, then this preference of drivers would be irrelevant since it would be the actual journey time that would be important. Introducing a multiplier to reflect congestion would increase the apparent economic benefits of investment aimed at reducing congestion, but it would be hard to justify increased public expenditure just to counter driver frustration.

4.6 Value of small time savings

For individual transport investments, time savings per person per trip are generally quite small, typically a few minutes. In SP experiments, it is commonly found that small time differences are valued less (per minute) than larger time differences. Moreover, losses of time (i.e. increases in journey time) are found to be valued more highly per minute than gains in time, an instance of what is known as 'loss aversion' (Daly 2021).

There has been debate about how to treat such small time savings (Daly, Tsang and Rohr 2014). On the one hand, it is argued that small amounts of time are of little value and are too insignificant to change travel behaviour, and so should be ignored. On the other hand, the view that has prevailed is that the accumulation of such small time savings from a succession of investments can have a substantial impact on behaviour and so in logic the components should not be disregarded.

The finding that the value of time savings (£/hour) increases with journey distance for business travel (Batley et al. 2017, 609) also prompts questions about logic, in that a given investment yielding a specific time saving will be valued differently by individuals according to the length of their journey. There is moreover a question of whether the value of time varies as a function of short-term versus long-term decisions, for instance for different routes for a single trip versus decisions about a change of workplace location. Beck et al. (2017) have presented evidence for higher values in the long term than in the short term.

Daly (2021) has observed that we do not have a good intuitive explanation of why small time savings are valued less per minute than larger time savings. He noted that values of time used in appraisal typically correspond to a journey time reduction of 10 minutes, which is a good deal longer than found in practice for most road schemes, so inflating the economic benefits. Daly concluded that the fundamental issue is that the economic theory required for appraisal excludes the behavioural effects that are required to explain the responses to SP surveys.

4.7 Induced traffic

In general, a reduction in the costs of travel on a route will lead to increased demand for travel since, prior to the reduction, some potential users will have been deterred by the cost. Costs comprise predominantly time costs, so that a road investment that increases capacity and reduces congestion delays must be expected to result in more traffic – known as 'induced traffic'. Such traffic may be attributed to a number of particular causes: longer trips by existing users to more distant destinations; existing users diverting to the new capacity to take advantage of faster travel, even if this involves a longer trip and increased vehicle operating costs (see section 5.4.1); from a change in mode of travel, as cost reduction increases the attraction of one mode over others; from new trips where faster travel makes travel to a desired destination possible where previously it would have taken the individual more time than was affordable; and in the longer run, from changes in land use arising from the greater access made possible by faster travel.

Hence induced traffic arises from both more trips and longer trips, and adds to detriments that are a function of vehicle-miles travelled (VMT): carbon and pollutant tailpipe emissions, traffic noise, deaths and injuries from collisions, all of which tend to be underestimated in conventional economic analysis based on time-saving. Induced traffic also adds to congestion, reducing travel time savings otherwise expected. But the additional trips that are made increase the access of users to desired destinations, which is in reality the main user benefit of transport investment.

Proponents of road investment have tended to minimise the scale of induced traffic since the additional traffic detracts from the travel time savings that would occur in its absence. The existence and origins of induced traffic have therefore been the subject of considerable debate (Goodwin 1996; Small 1999; Noland and Lem 2002; WSP 2018; Volker, Lee and Handy 2020). The thorough SACTRA (1994, para. 4.70) study suggested a short-term elasticity of demand with respect to travel time of the order of about –0.5, and a long-term elasticity of the order –1.0, implying that most time saved would be used for additional travel in the long run. Dunkerley, Rohr and Wardman (2021), reviewing the available evidence, found a wide range of elasticities reported for induced demand for road travel with respect to road capacity expansion, which vary with the type of intervention, level of congestion, how background traffic growth is controlled, and timescales: short-run estimates range from 0.03 to 0.6, long-run estimates from 0.16 to 1.39. This elasticity evidence is consistent with the expectation that there are more sources of induced demand in the long run, when changes in employment, residential location and land use may play a role, than in the short run.

The observed scale of induced traffic in relation to the time elapsed after scheme opening was investigated by Sloman, Hopkinson and Taylor (2017), based on published evaluations of 13 English road schemes, finding average increases in traffic over the short run (3–7 years) of 7 per cent and over the long run (8–20 years) of 47 per cent, all above background traffic growth. This study also looked in detail at four schemes, finding that road building was associated with highly car-dependent patterns of land development, such that increased road capacity led to housing developments in the countryside from which the vast majority of trips were by car, as well as the development of business parks and retail parks generating large numbers of vehicle movements causing serious congestion.

The US state of California has explicitly recognised the need to take account of induced traffic when considering proposals for increases in road capacity, and has sponsored a calculator that allows the estimation of the vehicle-miles of travel induced annually as a result of adding general-purpose or high-occupancy-vehicle-lane miles to state highways in urbanised counties (Caltrans 2020).

The findings of the National Travel Survey (see section 2.2) point clearly to the explanation of the main origin of induced traffic, which arises because in the long run people take the benefit of faster travel by travelling further, not by saving time. This extra traffic tends to restore congestion to what it had been before the investment, which is the basis for the maxim 'You can't build your way out of congestion,' which we know from experience to be generally true. Duranton and Turner (2011) analysed the relationship between US city-level traffic volumes and metropolitan highway capacity over time, leading these authors to postulate a 'fundamental law of road congestion', whereby road construction leads to a proportional increase in traffic in populated areas. Consistent with this finding, Garcia-López, Pasidis and Viladecans-Marsal (2022) analysed data from the 545 largest European cities for the relationship between congestion and highway expansion, finding an elasticity close to 1; this implied that expansion of the highway network induced demand for car travel, such that on average the level of congestion remained roughly unchanged in the period 1985–2005.

In principle, estimation of consumer surplus (see section 4.2) can include that arising from changing trip destinations (and travel modes) (Jara-Diaz 2007, 83). However, there then arises a problematic distinction between experienced and notional travel time savings.

Consider a trip initially between origin A and destination B along a single road. Suppose there is investment that allows faster travel, such that some travellers (Group 1) save time on their trip to B, while others (Group 2) now use what could have been time saved instead to continue to a further destination, C, where their needs are better satisfied than at B. There will also be those (Group 3) who did not initially travel at all, but after the investment now travel to B for the benefits gained there. Those in Group 1 experience a time-saving benefit arising from faster travel on an unchanged trip, while the benefit to those in Group 3 is set at half the time saving to Group 1 – the 'rule-of-a-half' (see section 4.2) – because new users cannot experience a benefit greater than the reduction in the cost of travel, nor less than zero, so their benefit is assumed to lie halfway between these extremes. However, the benefit to Group 2 is derived from the superior opportunities they access at the new destination, C, compared with what they had previously at destination B, without the experience of actual time saving. Nevertheless, it could be argued that the time saving they would have gained had they not gone on from B to C is a measure of the access benefit at C, since the latter must be more than the access benefit at B (if not, travel to C would not have occurred).

So, in this example, as a result of the investment that allows faster travel, there are real, experienced time savings for travellers in Group 1, no such change for those in Group 2, and additional travel time for those in Group 3. However, it could be argued that there are notional time savings for those in Groups 2 and 3, reflecting the additional benefits gained at the new destinations. The real gains and losses of travel time are broadly consistent with the invariance of average travel time, although the latter relates to all trips made, not just the single trip considered in the stylised example above. Thus, for instance, those in Group 3 may have travelled to destination B instead of a trip to a different destination.

This distinction between real and notional time savings is relevant to what may be observed when evaluating the outcome of transport investments. Short-run time savings can be observed for particular trips, most easily on timetabled rail journeys. But longer-run time savings that might be experienced by individuals are not generally measurable. Nor are notional time savings observable. The distinction between real and notional time savings is relevant when we come to consider transport modelling in the next chapter, since notional time savings cannot be accommodated in models that are intended to reflect observed travel behaviour.

4.8 Road traffic congestion

Congestion is a ubiquitous feature of road networks. Most road investment is intended to reduce congestion, with travel time savings as the main assumed benefit. Yet, as noted above, road investment that increases capacity, initially reducing congestion delays, must be expected to result in more traffic – induced traffic – tending to restore congestion to what it had been previously.

Congestion arises in or near densely populated urban areas where car ownership levels are high. There are more trips that could be made by car at times of peak usage than can be accommodated by the capacity of the network, such that some potential road users are deterred by the prospect of unacceptable delays. They may decide to use a different route or a different mode of travel where available, to travel at a time when there is less traffic or to a different destination where there are such options (shopping, for instance), or not to travel at all (such as by shopping online). The suppression of potential road use by the expectation of excessive delays is responsible for the self-regulating nature of congestion, in that if traffic grows and delays increase, more users are deterred. Hence the experience that in well-managed cities with alternative modes of travel available, gridlock is rare and generally arises from unexpected events (Metz 2021a; Litman 2022).

It is customary to distinguish between recurrent congestion that occurs when the road capacity is insufficient to accommodate the existing vehicle volume, and non-recurrent congestion that mainly results from collisions, disabled vehicles, bad weather, roadworks and special events. The impact of non-recurrent congestion depends on how close the road is to operating at full capacity. The perceived impact of both recurrent and non-recurrent congestion can be mitigated by digital navigation, as will be discussed (see section 7.3).

The existence of suppressed trips is the reason why attempts to reduce congestion tend to be unsuccessful. Adding road capacity reduces delays and so encourages previously suppressed trips to be made, adding to traffic and restoring congestion to what it had been, hence the maxim that you can't build your way out of congestion (Downs 1962; Ladd 2012). Interventions that seek to divert car users to other means of travel – such as public transport or the active modes of walking and cycling – free up carriageway space, which then becomes available for previously suppressed trips.

Transport economists have almost uniformly advocated road pricing (also known as road user charging or congestion charging) as the best means to mitigate congestion. The intention is to require each road user to take into account the marginal additional cost that they impose on other users arising from the increased delays resulting from their trip. If this cost is not experienced in the price paid by users, demand is excessive and congestion results.

Glaister (2018), in a review of UK experience, stated: 'Road user charging divides those with the economist's way of thinking from all others. To economists it is the obvious solution. To the others it is crazy.' Glaister recognised that the public acceptability of any road pricing scheme would depend on who would gain and who would lose and, in particular, the extent to which it is perceived to be 'fair', taking account of who pays and when, what happens to existing road taxation and who enjoys the benefits of any net revenues.

It is generally assumed that lower-income road users, who would be deterred from trips by a charge, would need to benefit from better public transport services made possible by the application of revenues from the charging scheme. Yet this is a political response, not an economic analysis. The economic effect of road user charging is to internalise what is otherwise an externality – the cost each road user imposes on others through adding to congestion delays. But in so doing, a new externality is generated – what might be termed 'the cost of inequity'.

Transport is a relatively egalitarian domain in that it is not easy to pay more to travel faster, as on trains and planes where a first-class ticket offers only superior comfort, and likewise for cars on roads subject to legal speed limits. Introduction of road pricing to lessen congestion, justified on grounds of economic efficiency, nevertheless diminishes the opportunity of those on lower incomes to use their vehicles when they would wish, hence adding to inequity. Inequity is a matter of increasing concern in society generally, so that proposals perceived as increasing this tend to generate public pushback.

The broad topic of transport and inequality has received attention (see section 1.6 and Banister 2018; Gates et al. 2019), and there has been analysis of survey findings of attitudes to 'fairness' of both road users and citizens in a number of cities, some with road user charging in operation (Eliasson 2017). Yet economic analysis of the cost of inequity seems not to have been addressed by transport economists. It is therefore possible that the net benefits of road pricing, when the cost of inequity is set against the efficiency benefits, may be a good deal smaller than generally supposed. If so, this would be consistent with the general reluctance of citizens to agree proposals for new road pricing schemes.

Although the concept of road pricing as a policy intervention to relieve congestion dates back to the 1964 report of a panel chaired by Reuben Smeed that had been commissioned by the UK Ministry of Transport (MoT 1964), it has been put into practice in only three major cities, London, Stockholm and Singapore (Metz 2018). Its possible role in relation of transport decarbonisation will be discussed later (see section 6.2.3).

4.9 Wider economic impacts

It is generally recognised that a change in the transport system leads to changes in accessibility, which in turn may lead to new development that contributes to changes in the real economy (SACTRA 1999; Mackie, Batley and Worsley 2018). The worth of such development may be observed as increases in values of land and property (real estate) made more accessible as a result of the transport investment. However, the standard approach to the economic appraisal of transport investments treats time savings to users as the main economic benefit. It is recognised that much of this user benefit may be transmitted through markets to other beneficiaries, so that the value of reductions in travel time is regarded as a proxy for the ultimate economic benefit of investment in a transport project, derived from reduced transport costs to industry, improved access to jobs, enhanced competition, development of property served by the transport project and so on (ITF 2019, 9).

For instance, an investment that permits faster travel on a rail route may allow users to commute from greater distances, resulting in an increase in house prices and rents in areas that now come within the new travel-to-work area, and hence windfall gains to property owners. It is therefore argued that to add such benefits to property owners to the benefits to transport users would amount to double counting, since what users are willing to pay is supposed to take account of the benefits from access to the destination, viewing transport as a means of overcoming distance. Similarly, firms whose transport costs fall may be able to increase their returns or may pass the benefits to consumers in a competitive market; again, to include these benefits to firms and consumers would be double counting the benefits estimated to transport users, it is claimed. This line of argument requires that markets in general are in a state of perfect competition, with constant returns to scale.

In reality, however, market failures arise where the price system fails to align benefits with costs, and moreover increasing returns to scale are possible; it is recognised that these give rise to economic impacts additional to user benefits. Transport investment enhances proximity, bringing firms and workers closer together (in economic terms). It may cause changes in the location of economic activity; households may move or change jobs and firms may relocate, changing the suppliers that they use or the markets to which they sell.

Venables (2021) distinguishes three kinds of economic impacts of transport improvements: first, direct benefits of the improvement in terms of vehicle operating costs, time savings and other benefits to existing and new users, together with the costs of noise and pollution produced. Then there are two kinds of wider impact: (a) the economic benefits deriving from better connectivity, holding constant the spatial distribution of economic activity; and (b) the changes in the location of economic activity arising as transport improvements change the spatial pattern of private-sector investment, such that new investments may be induced in some places, possibly at the expense of other places.

Venables, Laird and Overman (2014) have provided a clear summary of the basis for taking into account these wider economic impacts (see also Laird and Venables 2017 for further discussion). The main such wider economic benefits resulting from lower transport costs are increased numbers of people working in more productive jobs, and more competition between firms leading to lower costs to consumers. In addition to these 'static' effects, there are also 'dynamic' effects in that transport investment fosters the formation of clusters of economic and social activities, leading to greater scale and density, thus increasing productivity and innovation. This is seen in particular in large cities, which have developed to provide the benefits of 'agglomeration' – sharing, matching and learning: sharing of local infrastructure and other services as well as pools of specialised workers; matching of workers to jobs and suppliers of business services to customers; and learning through proximity to others – the knowhow that is 'in the air'. As well as businesses, agglomeration benefits consumers by sharing, matching and learning to enlarge consumer choice and opportunities. Transport is important both in allowing cities to grow and agglomerate, and also in connecting them to other locations for synergistic benefits (but see section 3.2 for discussion of the disbenefits of agglomeration).

In essence, the standard approach to the economic valuation of transport investments starts with the estimation of the user benefits arising from reduction in generalised costs of travel, of which travel time savings is the dominant element, to which are added such elements of the range of wider impacts as are relevant to the investment in question. As Venables, Laird and Overman (2014) discuss, there are considerable uncertainties involved in estimating values of the wider benefits, in part because agglomeration effects cannot be observed directly, which means that productivity benefits have to be estimated indirectly by means of econometric analysis. For example, transport investment can improve performance in imperfectly competitive markets, valued in the standard approach by applying a 10 per cent uplift to business user benefits (TAG Unit A2.2, 4.3.1, 2020). Yet Venables, Laird and Overman (2014, 28) suggest that this approach lacks context specificity and risks significant errors, and argue that application of the methodology is not sufficiently attuned to the specific project that is being studied. More generally, because of the uncertainties, estimation of the scale of wider economic impacts is prone to optimism bias.

The tacit assumption is that building on the supposedly firm base of user benefits, determined on the assumption of perfect markets, there can be added additional economic benefits arising from agglomeration and other impacts associated with market imperfections, albeit of uncertain magnitude. However, as discussed in section 4.2, the estimation of time-saving benefits is anything but firm, notably in respect of the use of values of travel time based on stated preference surveys offering immediate travel choices, the relationship of which to long-run values of access is quite tenuous. This relationship is especially shaky for large transformational transport investments for which wider economic impacts are expected to be greatest (Worsley 2021).

A detailed analysis of 15 case studies of transport investments, seeking evidence of transformational change, concluded that it is rare to find transport investments which, in isolation, change or reverse underlying economic or transport trends, with few instances of benefits realisation strategies being systematically developed to ensure the benefits ultimately materialise, and transformation seemingly requiring private investment to be levered in, potentially at a level several times the level of the original public investment (CEPA 2023). Coyle (2022) argues for an approach to appraisal that identifies when major projects have transformational potential, and an approach to policy that actively ensures complementary investments occur by tackling coordination failures either among different policy actors or between private- and public-sector activities. Generally, it may be concluded that transport investments considered in isolation cannot be counted on to lead to transformational change, whereas a co-ordinated effort by planners, developers and transport authorities has the potential to change land use on a sufficient scale to be transformational. The creation of New Towns in Britain after the Second World War is an example of transformational change, with Milton Keynes, the last of these, designed to accommodate traffic at a time when car ownership was growing. Another example is the recent extension of London Underground's Northern Line to Battersea, discussed in the following section, while the redevelopment of London's Docklands depended, albeit in a less co-ordinated way, on a succession of rail schemes – the Docklands Light Railway, the Jubilee Line Extension, the Overground and the Elizabeth Line (see section 4.16.1).

4.10 Land use

As noted in the previous section, transport investment can change how land is used and hence its economic value, whether by making land accessible for development or by increasing access to existing properties. The relationship between transport and land use was first recognised by Von Thünen, whose classic work related the value of agricultural land, as measured by the rents that farmers could afford to pay to landowners, to the costs of transporting the produce to the nearest market (Von Thünen 1826). This approach, relating land use, land value and transport costs within a spatial framework, was extended to urban situations (Alonso 1964) and forms part of urban economics (Tabuchi 2011; Duranton and Puga 2015).

Increased access made possible by transport investment may increase the value of both residential property and commercial premises (capital value and rental income), for instance on account of greater footfall for retail businesses. Changes in real estate values are affected by a range of other factors, of course, yet in many cases the impact of new transport facilities is observable as an uplift in market valuation in relation to an estimated counterfactual case of value in the absence of the investment. Such uplifts are most readily observed where transport investment makes underdeveloped agricultural or urban brownfield land accessible for residential or commercial development. Yet given the long-run invariance of average travel time, changes in access and land use must be a general consequence of transport investment. Nevertheless, the standard approach to transport investment appraisal assumes that land use changes are unlikely to be significant for the majority of schemes (TAG A2.1, 2.3.4 2019). Hence the standard approach disregards uplift in real estate values for the purposes of calculating the benefit–cost ratio, thereby avoiding the risk of double counting benefits, relying instead on notional travel time and money savings that are derived from models and not observable beyond the short run at best.

The best way of avoiding double counting of benefits is for their estimation to be based on observable evidence. If users are taking advantage of a faster journey to travel further, they cannot benefit from the saving of travel time, and vice versa. Accordingly, it is worth considering the scope for recognising uplift in real estate values as the prime basis for the appraisal of investments, not least because the notional reduction in generalised costs is never the policy objective of the investment.

The UK Department for Levelling Up, Housing and Communities (formerly known as the Department for Communities and Local Government) does not have the fixation on transport user benefits that determines the focus of the Department for Transport. It therefore straightforwardly recognises that change in land value as a result of a change in land use from a development reflects the economic efficiency benefits of converting land into a more productive use. Accordingly, land value data should be the primary means of assessing the benefits of a development, not least because such data is a rich source of information reflecting market data on individuals' and firms' willingness to pay for a piece of land (DLUHC 2023).

There have been a number of studies where the value of transport-induced changes in land value have been estimated ex post. Jones et al. (2004) evaluated how the regeneration of London's Docklands (the former port area) depended on public investment to extend the Jubilee Line, a rail route that made this brownfield land more accessible, so that private-sector developers could construct commercial and residential property to accommodate London's growth. Gibbons and Machin (2003) found that residential house prices in the vicinity of stations on the Jubilee Line Extension and Docklands Light Railway increased by 9.3 per cent compared to places unaffected by these infrastructure changes. Banister and Thurstain-Goodwin (2011) estimated that the Jubilee Line Extension added £2.2 billion to property values in the vicinity of stations. Song et al. (2019) also estimated house price increases associated with an extension of the Docklands Light Railway.

More generally, Mohammad et al. (2013) carried out a meta-analysis of the impact of 23 rail projects on land and property values, finding a wide range of outcomes, dependent on contextual and methodological factors. Grimes and Liang (2010) used changes in land values to estimate the benefit–cost ratio of an extension to a motorway in Auckland, New Zealand. Lee, Lim and Leong (2018) have shown that the benefits of a new rail line in Singapore, as estimated from property value uplift and intensification, were greater than conventional time savings and other user benefits. Sharma and Newman (2018) found substantial increases in property values in Bangalore associated with the construction of an urban rail route. Knowles and Ferbrache (2016) reviewed international experience of the wider economic impact of light rail schemes on cities, including land and property value increase, concluding that such impacts can be positive, but that light rail investment alone is unlikely to be a sufficient catalyst for economic change without additional supportive policies.

In contrast to these ex-post studies, there appears to be only a limited number of published cases that attempt to justify investment by ex-ante forecasts of increase in real estate values. A study of the impact of proposed new river crossings in East London identified all major development sites within the relevant area and assessed the scope for development as this would be affected by the increased access to labour, customers and suppliers (TfL 2014). Outputs were stated as increases in numbers of residential units and area of floor space for non-residential property. Although no attempt was made to ascribe monetary values to these developments, that would be a natural next step to facilitate an economic appraisal of the proposed river crossings based on expected changes in land use and real estate values. Although the proposed river crossings were not constructed, this example illustrates how the outcome of decisions to make transport investments depends on decisions by planners and developers. The conventional approach to transport economic appraisal that disregards changes in land use simplifies the modelling and analysis, at the cost of failing to inform decision makers about the nature of the ultimate benefits.

A second forward-looking example from London is the extension of the Northern Line underground rail route to a large brownfield site at Battersea at a cost of £1 billion, to which the developers contributed a quarter as cash and additional taxes to be paid by businesses locating to the area allowed TfL to borrow the remainder (known as tax incremental financing) (Porter 2014). This followed an earlier appraisal of a range of alternative property and transport investments, which identified extension of the underground as necessary if high density development were desired, with the developer contributing to the cost (TfL 2009; see also section 4.16.1).

A third case of ex-ante assessment of land use change is cited by DfT as an example of good practice. A proposed new local access road to the port of Newhaven, East Sussex, had a low benefit–cost ratio (BCR) based on transport user benefits. Since the intention of the scheme was to unlock the town's economic growth potential, modelling was used to estimate commercial floorspace expected to be created, the employment consequences, and likely displacement of employment from elsewhere. Taking account of these land use changes increased the BCR to medium-high value for money (DfT 2021d).

The UK National Infrastructure Commission commissioned a study of how land values respond to changes in land use and infrastructure improvements, as a basis for informing future investment decisions. Comprehensive property databases were drawn upon to model how prices depend on property characteristics and location. This enabled creation of a web-based 'property value uplift' tool that could be used to calculate how values and rents of existing properties would respond to small-scale investments in roads or public transport, and also values for prospective new settlements (Halket et al. 2019). A similar study quantified the relationship between transport and property values in the North of England with a view to inclusion in the case for new investment (Nellthorp et al. 2019).

Simmonds (2023) has developed an approach to transport investment appraisal in which the main calculation of economic benefits is based on measures of improvement in accessibility, explicitly reflecting both transport conditions and the distribution of land uses, rather than on time or cost savings for specific journeys as in standard transport appraisal. This has been implemented in a dynamic land-use/transport-interaction model.

A current policy objective in Britain is the desirability of making transport investments that would make land accessible for new housing, to help accommodate a growing population (DCLG 2017). This has prompted consideration of methodology to capture the housing benefits of transport investment (DfT 2019b, 6.7–6.10). Although the standard approach to transport appraisal does not include the uplift in real estate values in calculating the BCR, such uplift may be taken into account by decision makers in judging the value for money of the investment (DfT 2018a). More generally, while it is recognised that the impacts of transport investment are spatially dispersed, spatial analysis is treated as supplementary to cost–benefit analysis based on generalised cost reduction (TAG A4.3, 2022).

Disregard of uplift in real estate value is problematic, however, as an example may illustrate. Consider a proposal to construct a bypass around a town experiencing traffic congestion. The conventional economic case would be based mainly on travel time savings plus accident savings and reduced vehicle operating costs. However, the new road may make agricultural land available for development, in which case developers may seek planning consent to build new houses. If consent were granted by the planners, the economic case for the road would be very different from what it would be without consent, as regards both traffic flows and the nature and scale of the economic benefits. It would not be credible to argue that the additional economic value of the new houses would be captured in the time savings of the scheme without the housing.

The implication of travel time invariance is that transport investments would generally result in changes in land use. Decisions on such investments should therefore not be taken in isolation but in a tripartite collaboration involving planners, developers and transport authorities, where related development could be taken into account. Addressing how changes in land use and values are affected by transport investment is relevant to the possibility of capturing some of the uplift in value that could be used to help fund the investment, a topic of increasing interest (Medda 2012; Higgins and Kanaroglou 2016; TfL 2017).

More generally, the sub-discipline of spatial economics aims to explain why there are peaks and troughs in the spatial distribution of wealth and people, as the result of both attractive forces, which lead to the concentration of economic activities, and dispersive forces that bring about the spreading of economic activities at regional and urban levels. Transport matters at both scales: the interregional flows of goods and passenger trips at the regional level and individual commuting at the urban level. Proost and Thisse (2019) illuminatingly discuss these aspects that are crucial for transport analysis, observing that the literature in spatial economics has paid too little attention to what has been accomplished in transportation economics, and vice versa. Venables, Laird and Overman (2014) recognised the case for calculating the impact of transport investment on the spatial pattern of activity, and noted a number of possible approaches: bottom-up, based on local knowledge and plans of the likely consequences of new transport provision; land-use transport-interaction models; and spatial equilibrium models (to be considered in the next chapter).

4.11 Transport investment and economic development

Aside from the relationship between transport investment and land-use change, there is the question of how investment contributes to economic development, generally an important objective of policy. Where continued development of an economically vibrant city is constrained by crowding on public transport and congestion on roads, investment may be justified to permit growth to continue. This has been the basis for investment in London's rail network in recent decades. The National Infrastructure Commission has proposed a methodology to appraise the likely benefits of urban transport investments (see section 4.16.1).

However, evidence is limited and mixed for the way in which transport investment can promote economic growth in regions where the economy is less dynamic. A systematic evaluation of the local economic impact of transport investments found, inter alia, that while road projects can positively impact local employment, effects are not always positive and a majority of evaluations showed no (or mixed) effects on employment; moreover, such projects may increase firm entry, either through new firms starting up or existing firms relocating, but this does not necessarily increase the overall number of businesses since new arrivals may displace existing firms (What Works Centre for Local Economic Growth 2015). Gibbons (2017) similarly concluded that claims that big transport infrastructure investment is a cost-effective way of generating new growth either nationally or regionally should be treated with some caution; while compelling as a policy option, it is a hard one to be confident about based on the evidence.

Docherty and Waite (2018), reviewing the relevant literature, concluded that decades of research have not been able to pin down the causal relationships between transport investments and economic performance as effectively as policymakers might like. Marshall and Dumbaugh (2020) analysed 30 years of data from 89 US metropolitan areas to evaluate the economic impacts of road traffic congestion, finding that economic productivity is not significantly negatively impacted by high levels of congestion. Laird and Johnson (2021), reviewing both theory and experience, concluded that transport investment is a destabilising force, as by changing transport costs the balance between regions and countries is changed; this can lead to productivity gains from agglomeration and specialisation, but is also likely to lead to reorganisation and displacement effects. For an interregional transport investment, economic activity may shift either to the lower-productivity region (the periphery) or to the higher-productivity region (the core), depending on the underlying economic conditions and the type and scope of the investment.

Leunig (2011), reviewing key historic case studies of transport investments, concluded that while big transport breakthroughs – such as replacing walking with railways, or creating a highway network for the first time – do have big effects, these are unlikely to be seen again in developed economies; instead, transport is best regarded as having a supporting role such that as long as the transport system is 'good enough', the returns to greater investment will be relatively limited. So the economic case for transport investment to stimulate growth in economically lagging regions is far from clear-cut, notwithstanding the political popularity of such investment, at least when funded by central government.

Blagden and Tanner (2021) note the conventional wisdom that the UK's economic history is characterised by periods of rapid growth driven by successive connectivity revolutions: the canal network in the eighteenth century, the railway network in the nineteenth century and the road network in the twentieth century; all three coincided with sharp increases in national productivity. These authors' granular analysis of current connectivity leads to the conclusion that regional differences in income are far better explained by qualification levels and the mix of occupations and industries than by connectivity to jobs, so that further transport investments won't do much to improve incomes and living standards in a place without addressing other economic fundamentals such as education and the quality of jobs available. Yet weak connectivity may be holding back growth in specific parts of the UK.

4.12 Access

As noted in section 4.3, there is an emerging shift in focus in transport investment appraisal, from a mobility perspective involving travel time savings and congestion relief, to achieving better access to employment, goods, activities and other opportunities. In the former view, additional travel through cost reduction is generally seen as necessarily yielding additional welfare. From the latter perspective, travel is considered a derived demand, and its underlying purpose of increasing effective access to goods, services and activities may be met in ways other than travel. However, while time savings and related mobility-associated concepts are easily understood, in contrast, there is no pre-eminent accessibility indicator that is widely accepted as the appropriate starting point for project appraisal practice (ITF 2020).

An access, or accessibility, perspective necessitates a holistic view of transport and land use since decisions made under each framework affect the outcomes of the other. Indeed, a focus on one appraisal framework while disregarding the other can be counter-productive, as when increased highway capacity results in urban sprawl, which reduces access for those not able to use a car. (Also to be taken into account is virtual access, the result of the general use of the internet for access to consumption and many other kinds of opportunity [Lyons 2002], as exemplified by the changes during the coronavirus pandemic discussed in the previous chapter, although this perspective has yet to illuminate the traditional discussion, considered next.)

The question that arises is how to make the concept of access operational, in particular how to attribute a monetary value, to allow the economic value of improved access to be recognised in cost–benefit analysis.

The concepts of access and accessibility have received considerable attention, with a variety of methodologies identified for quantifying improvements. Handy (2020) has summarised the problematic history of the concept. A comprehensive *Transport Access Manual* (2020) is available, prepared by an expert committee. The underlying concept is that access needs can be met by movement (mobility), but can also be assisted by how the built environment is structured. (Access, or accessibility, in this context, is distinct from concern about access to the supply of transport, for instance how far people live from a bus stop or whether those with disabilities can board a train; bus stops and railway stations are interim, not final destinations.)

Geurs and Van Wee (2004) adopted the term 'access' when considering a person's perspective, and 'accessibility' for a location's perspective. Both depend on the pattern of land use and transport provision, and reflect the needs of individuals and the time constraints under which they operate. Geurs and Van Wee identified four approaches to quantifying accessibility: (i) measures of performance of the transport system, such as speed on a road network, a traditional perspective of transport professionals who see low speeds as limiting access; (ii) measures that reflect access to opportunities from particular locations, such as the number of jobs within 30 minutes' travel time from origin locations; (iii) person-based measures, reflecting the activities in which an individual can participate in a given time; and (iv) utility-based measures that reflect the economic benefits gained by individuals from access to spatially distributed activities.

Utility-based measures of accessibility are in principle appropriate for the appraisal of proposed transport investments. What are known as random utility discrete choice transport models allow estimation of the maximum utility or benefit achievable from the choices available to individuals (sometimes known as 'logsum' values, reflecting the mathematical form). This benefit can be related to traditional consumer surplus measures (Fosgerau and Pilegaard 2021). However, the theory is relatively complex and in consequence this approach has not been generally employed in practice. Importantly, as Geurs and Van Wee (2004) note, utility-based measures show diminishing returns, consistent with the evidence for travel demand saturation (see section 2.5), and in contrast to travel time savings for which diminishing returns are not assumed. Venter (2016) reviewed utility-based measures of accessibility, identifying only a few examples of their use in practice (for example Geurs et al. 2010). He attributed this to their dependence on complex destination/mode choice models in combination with integrated land use/transport models, neither in common use – a challenge in respect of both cost and communication to decision makers. Silva et al. (2017) investigated why accessibility instruments are not widely used in practice, concluding that the main impediments were lack of user-friendliness and institutionalisation, as well as organisational barriers.

Duranton and Guerra (2016) argue for the centrality of accessibility in thinking about urban development since it links land use, housing and transportation. They view urban transportation infrastructure as a congestible public good, and observe that commercial development, firm location and household location decisions are all subject to externalities. For instance, a household's decision to move to a neighbourhood directly affects the well-being of neighbours through social interactions, peer effects and investments that the household may or may not make in its house, as well as use of local public services, transport and others. Hence accessibility emerges as the outcome of choices made by firms and residents. However, a theory of urban locations where both residents and firms would choose their locations remains elusive. While the simplest stylised models yield transparent results, changes to assumptions to reflect realism increase both complexity and the sensitivity of outcomes to place-dependent factors such as urban amenity or the cost of travel.

Accordingly, while improved access is the main user benefit resulting from transport investment, quantification and monetisation within a coherent theoretical framework has proved difficult, with little application in practice. Yet the expected diminishing returns from access are consistent with evidence for travel demand saturation, as discussed previously (section 2.5). The orthodox approach to transport economic analysis, focused on the saving of travel time, disregards the possibilities of demand saturation and hence justifies nugatory expenditure.

4.13 Diversity

Users of the transport system are a heterogeneous collection of individuals. Clearly, economic analysis cannot deal with individuals, so must lump them together according to common characteristics. More granularity in grouping allows more refined analysis, but at the cost of complexity and effort.

The standard approach to transport economic appraisal employs values of travel time that vary according to mode of travel and journey purpose. Current UK specification for national average values per hour of travel time saving for those travelling on business includes: rail, £29; car, £18; bus, walking and cycling, £10.[1] This range of values in part reflects the different income classes of individuals adopting the different modes of travel for business purposes. In contrast, for non-work travel, the standard approach employs national average values of time that do not depend on mode of travel: commuting, £10 per hour, and other trips, £5. Were values of time to be based on individuals' willingness to pay (behavioural values) that are related to income, then investment decisions would be biased towards those that benefit travellers with higher incomes. Investment would then be concentrated into high-income areas or travel modes, and the interests of those on lower incomes, who may already suffer from relatively lower mobility and accessibility, would be given less weight. For this reason, the policy of the UK DfT is to use national average values in transport appraisal (TAG A1.3, 4.3.4, 2022). On the other hand, behavioural values of time may be used for modelling purposes, with the aim of better reflecting actual user behaviour.

Notwithstanding the use of national average values of time in appraisal, there has been concern that less prosperous parts of the country have received less than a fair share of transport investment. Coyle and Sensier (2020) have argued that the standard appraisal methodology reinforces existing regional imbalance, a view disputed by Gonzales-Pampillon and Overman (2020). A review by the Treasury of its Green Book in 2020 admitted that current appraisal practice risked undermining the government's ambition to 'level up' poorer regions, in large part because of failure by scheme proposers to engage properly with the strategic context, including how places differ in the social and economic features and how the intervention may affect them (HMT 2020). The Green Book was subsequently amended to respond to criticisms, including placing emphasis on analysis of place-based impacts and on transformational change. Nevertheless, formulation of the strategic case remains problematic, as will be discussed later in section 4.17.

Other impacts that may be distributed unevenly across social groups are treated qualitatively in the UK DfT's approach to appraisal of interventions. Such groups include children, older people, people with a disability, Black and minority ethnic (BME) communities, people without access to a car and people on low incomes (TAG A4.2, 2020). The output of analysis of each of the expected impacts of interventions on each social group takes the form of short qualitative statements, with summaries reflecting the degree to which these are beneficial or adverse. However, these considerations do not contribute to the economic analysis of transport interventions.

4.14 Externalities

Besides the benefits to users of transport investments or other interventions, there are additional impacts, the costs of which are not borne by users but may be borne by others, known as externalities. A number of these have monetary values attributed, so can be included in the standard cost–benefit analysis. The monetised environmental impacts include noise, air quality and greenhouse gases. In contrast, other environmental impacts are treated qualitatively: landscape, townscape, historic environment, biodiversity and water environment (TAG A3, 2022). These latter impacts are not taken into account in cost–benefit analysis, although decision makers may be advised of the expected magnitudes of the effects.

Greenhouse gas emissions are of particular importance, given that the transport sector is responsible for around a quarter of all the UK's emissions and that demanding targets have been set for rapid decarbonisation (see Chapter 6). It is recognised that the impacts of proposed transport schemes on greenhouse gas emissions over their whole lifecycle must be incorporated within appraisal in a consistent and transparent way, and that the monetary value of such impacts of must be calculated. Whole-lifecycle carbon impacts comprise those emissions arising from the related increase in use, together with those associated with scheme construction, operation and maintenance. Monetary values of the standard unit, 'tonnes of carbon dioxide equivalent', have been set to be consistent with national targets for greenhouse gas reduction (DBEIS 2021) – to be further discussed in Chapter 6.

Road traffic collisions give rise to casualties, very largely involving cars and larger vehicles, to the detriment of both users of those vehicles and pedestrians and cyclists. From the perspective of the driver, the impact on other road users is an externality. Interventions that effect a reduction in casualties are of value in that human costs (pain, grief, suffering and the intrinsic loss of enjoyment of life) are avoided, as is loss of economic output due to injury (TAG A4.1, 2022). Current prescribed UK values are: for an avoided fatality, £1.7 million; serious injury, £180,000; and slight injury, £14,000.[2] The main component of these values reflects investigations of vehicle drivers' 'willingness to pay' to avoid being killed or injured (see Hensher et al. 2009 for discussion of methodologies). Availability of such monetary values allows the value of casualty reduction to be estimated from traffic models, comparing with- and without-intervention cases, values that can be incorporated into cost–benefit analysis of transport investments and other interventions.

There are other externalities that are taken into account in the appraisal of transport investments and interventions: security of transport users, severance of communities that result from changes to transport infrastructure or traffic flows, quality of the journey as experienced while travelling and personal affordability. For some of these, monetary values can be estimated, while for others only a qualitative treatment is possible (TAG A4.1, 2022).

The quantification of externalities depends on the validity of the transport models used to compare with- and without-investment cases. There is a general tendency to underestimate induced traffic, the additional traffic that results from increased road capacity (see section 4.7). Underestimation of traffic growth will mean underestimation of externalities. As an example, an estimate of the economic value of casualties arising from the additional accidents attributed to induced traffic for a range of UK highway schemes found that, on average, the loss of value from these additional accidents exceeded the value of accident savings claimed for these schemes (Metz 2006).

Road traffic congestion is an externality in that an individual's decision to use a congested road network imposes a cost on all other users. As with other externalities discussed above, the magnitude of which increases with vehicle-miles travelled, induced traffic adds to vehicle-miles travelled and thus to congestion. The public justification for road investment along a heavily used route is often expressed as an intent to reduce congestion and improve connectivity between cities – a proposition undermined by the traffic induced by the increase in capacity.

Agglomeration and other wider impacts, discussed previously (section 4.9), are positive externalities, unlike those considered above that are negative externalities and detract from net benefits.

4.15 Active travel

A positive feature of active travel, walking and cycling, is the health benefit to those using these modes. Woodcock, Givoni and Morgan (2013) found that shifting urban trips from car travel to walking and cycling can provide substantive benefits to population health, with the largest benefits attributed to reductions in ischaemic heart disease. The World Health Organization has developed a methodology for estimating the value of health benefits from active travel (WHO 2017). Based on this analysis, the UK DfT recommends appraising health impacts of active travel by estimating the change in premature death (mortality) resulting from a change in numbers of walkers and cyclists and their benefits from gaining more life years (TAG A4.1, 2022). It is therefore possible to derive economic impacts associated with such reduction in mortality by using the monetary values summarised in the previous section. These can be incorporated into cost–benefit analysis (TAG A5.1, 2022).

Van Wee (2021b) has noted the lack of adequate models and high-quality data for cycling economic appraisal, as well as limited insights of several quantitative effects and their monetary valuation.

There appears to be little consideration of situations where new cycle lanes are fitted to existing roads, such that less space is available for buses and other vehicles, with resulting increased delays and increased journey times that, in economic terms, would offset the value of the benefits of cycling. In the case of one proposed cycle route in London, it was estimated that the monetary value of the health and other benefits to cyclists would be exceeded by the journey time disbenefits to other traffic, but the scheme went ahead nevertheless (TfL 2013, 4.10).

There is also uncertainty about the extent to which new cycling facilities attract users away from car travel. A study of the impact of new cycle schemes in eight UK cities found that only 5 per cent of cyclists said they would have travelled by car if the scheme had not been built, although most users had cycled before implementation of the new schemes (Sloman et al. 2021, 10.3). The DfT's guidance, based on a literature review (Clark and Parkin 2022), stipulates a car-cycle diversion factor of 0.24, meaning that if there were to be 100 new cyclists, there would be 24 fewer people travelling by car (TAG A5.1, 3.7.3, 2022). The corollary is that 76 per cent would switch from other modes, largely from buses and walking. There is evidence from European cities with high bicycle use that this mode is mainly an alternative to public transport (see section 1.3.1). Reviewing the available literature, Teixeira, Silva and Moura e Sá (2021) concluded that bike-sharing is mostly replacing sustainable modes of transport, with modest car replacement rates.

4.16 Investments

The application of the considerations discussed above may be illustrated by reference to a number of UK transport investments for which sufficient documentation is available.

4.16.1 Rail investments

Crossrail is a major extension to London's Underground rail system that opened in 2022, when it was renamed the Elizabeth Line. The route comprises 13 miles of twin-bore tunnels under Central London, together with surface routes extending to the east and west of the city.

Worsley (2014) has provided a comprehensive account of the development of both the Crossrail project and its economic justification. The case for investment was based on the value of travel time savings to users (business, commuting and leisure) plus a number of wider economic impacts (mainly agglomeration benefits). The value of time saving benefits was put at £12,832 million, while the wider impacts provided an additional £7,159 million (DfT 2005). Subsequently, further analysis increased the wider benefits to £10–15 billion (Buchanan 2018).

However, there was no explicit reference in the investment case to the impact of the new rail route on real estate values or on the economic value of the businesses to be accommodated in new developments along the route. The assumption was that the boost to development and employment was accounted for by the value of travel time savings plus the wider impacts, an assumption that is scarcely credible to non-economists. Importantly, the economic analysis of the investment case failed to consider the spatial distribution of benefits, although by the very nature of the project, these would be largely within London.

Transport for London has developed a framework to evaluate the benefits of the Crossrail investment. It is envisaged that a study to be published two years after opening will address the transport effects of the new railway, including mode shift from cars to public transport, relief of congestion on public transport and roads, and the implications for air pollution and carbon emissions. A subsequent study is planned to consider the broader social and economic effects, including the effect of improved connectivity on new homes and jobs, changing patterns of employment and land use, and residential and commercial property prices (TfL 2022b). A report has been published on the pre-opening impacts of Crossrail on property prices, arising from the announcement of the project; this found fairly small positive increases to both house prices and office rents (Arup 2022).

This approach to evaluation is admirably ambitious, yet there is inconsistency with the original investment case, which was based on the value of notional travel time savings and of wider impacts inferred from econometric analysis, with no indication of the spatial distribution of benefits. It seems unlikely that it will prove possible to compare forecast and outturn by deducing time savings and agglomeration benefits from the evaluation findings, as would be desirable to assess the validity of the modelling in support of the investment decision. There is also the question of whether, with hindsight, the investment appraisal could have been based on projections of the actual benefits that are expected to be achieved.

The possibility of forecasting the actual expected benefits of investment is illustrated by another London rail investment, the Northern Line extension to a large brownfield site discussed earlier (section 4.10), where the developers contributed a quarter of the construction cost in cash, and additional taxes paid by businesses locating in the area will finance the remainder. The investment decision followed a standard economic appraisal of transport user benefits for a range of alternative property and transport investments, where the predominant benefits were travel time savings. It was found that extension of the Underground would have a less favourable benefit–cost ratio than other transport alternatives on account of the higher capital cost (TfL 2009, Table 28). Nevertheless, the decision was made to extend the Tube, the increase in real estate value being the deciding factor. Thus, the decision was taken essentially on a commercial basis, with the estimated increase in real estate value forming an integral element of the investment decision, exemplifying the scope for a transport authority working with a developer to take into account the value of real estate improvement. In this case, of an underground electric railway, detrimental externalities were not important.

High Speed 2 (HS2) is a new rail route under construction, intended to provide faster connections between London and the cities of the Midlands and the North of England. The scheme has been controversial on account of the high construction cost, which has increased at each stage of refinement of plans, as well as the environmental impact and uncertainty of benefits, both magnitude and spatial distribution (Glaister 2021). The increase in cost led to the route north of Birmingham being truncated in late 2023 (see below). The business case, published in 2020, set out the key strategic principles underpinning the investment, needed because the capacity of the existing rail network was not expected to cope with the projected growth in demand for rail travel; moreover, HS2 was intended to be a transformational programme that would act as a catalyst for wider growth and help level up the economies of the Midlands and the North (DfT 2020a).

Growth of demand for rail travel has been impacted by the coronavirus pandemic, as discussed in Chapter 3. Here, we consider the pre-pandemic economic case for HS2, which concluded that the benefit–cost ratio was no better than 1.5, representing 'low to medium value for money' according to the DfT's categorisation. The main BCR components for the full scheme were estimated as £74 billion present value for transport user benefits plus £20 billion for wider economic impacts, to be set against capital costs of £78 billion and operating costs of £25 billion (DfT 2020a, Table 2.9). The main elements of transport user benefit (present value) were estimated as: reduction in journey time, £39 billion; reduction in crowding, £13.5 billion; reduction in waiting, £9 billion; and greater reliability, £12 billion (DfT 2020a, Table 2.12). These numbers were regarded as fluid, depending particularly on assumptions made about the extent of the route, capital costs and travel demand growth; but they included the benefits to users of other parts of the rail network for which HS2 would relieve capacity constraints.

As with Crossrail, the assumption was that the transport user benefits, which account for the main part of total benefits, provide a good estimate of the ultimate benefits seen as the development of property and new businesses that occupy such real estate. This is a particularly problematic assumption since the distribution of benefits between London and the cities of the Midlands and the North was not attempted in the economic appraisal of the investment – and indeed is a difficult matter to predict.

Consider, for instance, a business with headquarters in London and a branch office in Birmingham. It might take advantage of the faster rail connection offered by HS2 by closing the branch office, serving clients in Birmingham from London; or it might expand the Birmingham branch where office rents and housing costs are lower, on the basis that staff could get up to the head office speedily as necessary; or arrangements may be left unchanged, with staff benefiting from the faster business travel spending more time in the office; and, of course, the increase in working from home as a result of the pandemic must influence all the possible business decisions. This is an instance of what is known as the 'two-way road effect', whereby improved accessibility between two regions may benefit prosperous areas rather than the poor areas targeted by the scheme (TAG A4.3, 1.4, 2022).

Given that the intention of HS2 is to boost the economies of cities and region to the north of London, uncertainty about distribution of economic benefits means that the value of the investment was always hard to judge. Much would depend on the ability of the connected cities to take advantage of the new rail route to put in place city-centre development around new stations plus local transport infrastructure to speed travellers to and from their final destinations. The HS2 business case included at Annex A an outline of hoped-for developments around the new Curzon Street station in Birmingham, which illustrates the possibilities. But these did not constitute part of the economic case for the investment, to avoid double counting. Yet again, notional time savings are preferred to estimates of real-world benefits when applying the orthodox methodology to the appraisal of transport investments.

In October 2023 the government announced that the high-speed track would not proceed past Birmingham on account of the increase in costs. Trains using the London to Birmingham sector would utilise existing track to travel further north. The money saved would be reallocated to a variety of other local transport investments of more immediate benefit.

Arguably, the failure of the economic analysis to estimate the real-world benefits and their distribution contributed to the decision to truncate HS2, in particular the treatment of the business case as a standalone transport investment, rather than the transport investment facilitating real estate investment and the resulting boost to economic activity.

In Sweden, preparation to implement high-speed rail links between the three largest cities involved inviting local governments along the possible routes to take part in the planning and financing of the project, with details to be settled in negotiation. In principle, this would be a means to maximise overall benefits. In practice, however, the analyses of benefits prepared by local government bodies proved to be inconsistent, lacking comparability and prone to optimism bias, likely because of the role of such analyses in a negotiation process (Ronnie 2017). Nevertheless, with clearer guidance to achieve consistency and minimise optimism bias, such a collaborative approach would have attractions.

One feature of the HS2 business case is consideration of a variant case in which the economic benefits were estimated out to 100 years from opening, in contrast to the standard 60-year time horizon (TAG A1.1, 2021). The effect is to increase the BCR significantly. The rationale is that while the mechanical and electrical elements of the rail route would have asset lives of less than 60 years, the earthworks, bridges and tunnels would be expected to last for longer. Following publication of the HS2 business case, the DfT consulted on the length of appraisal periods generally; a majority of respondents argued against extending on account of both the practical difficulties of forecasting out this far, and the realism of such practice in the face of significant uncertainty, including a credible representation of the without-investment scenario. Moreover, a study commissioned by the Department into the long-term benefits of transport schemes questioned the practicality of running transport models far into the future, noting uncertainties about drivers of travel demand and user benefits over such timescales (Arup 2016). Nevertheless, the Department took the view that a longer appraisal period should not be precluded in cases where this could be justified (DfT 2021b, 25). Seemingly, appraisal period extension, as in the instance of HS2, reflects an attempt to better align the analytical outcome with a prior political decision of the benefits of the investment.

The UK government's Integrated Rail Plan for the North and the Midlands (DfT 2021a) was mentioned earlier on account of its recognition that people have taken the benefits of better transport links as the ability to access a wider range of jobs, business and leisure opportunities, rather than to reduce total time spent travelling (see section 4.3). The plan included consideration of options for improved east–west connectivity between the cities of the North of England, all of which were assessed as low to poor value for money. The plan recognised that: 'Rail schemes in the North are at increased risk of being considered poor value for money when applying conventional cost–benefit analysis. This is driven in part by smaller city populations in the North, different travel patterns, as well as the general high cost of building rail infrastructure' (DfT 2021a, 98). This admission of the failure of standard economic analysis to confirm the politically desired investment programme necessitated recourse to an alternative methodology. As Groucho Marx said: 'Those are my principles, and if you don't like them . . . well, I have others.'

The alternative methodology that informed the Integrated Rail Plan had been developed by the National Infrastructure Commission, whose role is to advise on investment in all national infrastructure. The Commission was asked to prepare an assessment of the rail needs of the Midlands and the North; this proposed priority for regional links as having the highest potential economic benefits, rather than long distance links (NIC 2020). The Commission used a multi-criteria approach to assess the options, including quantification of the economic benefits both from improving business productivity in city centres and from connecting people to city-centre services. This approach drew upon a previous study addressing how to capture the value of urban transport investments, which recognised the invariance of average travel time and so looked for the real benefits arising from increased city density made possible by investment in urban transport. Agglomeration benefits to business have long been recognised. The Commission's novel approach was to replace the orthodox transport user benefits with amenity benefits based on the social value increased by thriving and densifying cities (NIC 2019). The government broadly followed the Commission's advice in formulating its Integrated Rail Plan.

For rail investments, which are often politically high profile, decision making is influenced by expected real-world outcomes far more than by the findings of economic analysis based largely on the supposed value of notional travel time savings. The implications of this conclusion will be further discussed in the final chapter.

4.16.2 Road investments

The A303 is a road connecting London and the South-East to the South-West of England, used by both longer-distance and local travellers. This historic route comprises a mixture of single-lane (in each direction) and dual-carriageway roads. One of the single-lane sections runs close to the Stonehenge ancient monument, designated as a World Heritage Site.

A plan has been developed to sink a section of the road in a two-mile tunnel costing close to £1 billion. However, user benefits from faster travel have been estimated to amount to only £250 million present value. To make the scheme at all economically viable, with a break-even BCR of about 1, 'cultural heritage' benefits of almost £1 billion have been invoked (Highways England 2018, Table 6.1).

The estimation of cultural benefits was based on a stated preference survey designed to elicit monetary values for a hypothetical change in noise, tranquillity, visual amenity and landscape severance within the Stonehenge area, by asking individuals about their willingness to pay for, or willingness to accept monetary compensation for, a hypothetical change in the layout of the A303 road (Highways England 2017). Based on 3,500 survey responses, it was estimated that the cultural benefits to visitors to the site were worth £25 million present value; benefits to users of the road, £50 million; and to the general population, £1.2 billion. However, the very high monetary value attributed to cultural benefits is both unusual and problematic in that there must be very considerable uncertainty about such an estimation. The question is whether people might have responded with a higher value than they would have done in a real-life decision-making situation. This case could be said to be another example of the economic analysis being devised to fit a prior political decision.

The A303 Stonehenge scheme has been the subject of a review by the National Audit Office (NAO), whose role is to provide independent scrutiny of public spending (NAO 2019). This review recognised that the Stonehenge scheme was only one of eight projects aimed at upgrading the route corridor, yet no overarching programme-level business case had been produced; the DfT and its wholly owned subsidiary, Highways England, intend to seek approval for each project individually. However, based on the standard appraisal process, five of the uncommitted projects along the corridor are rated as low to poor value for money, which means there must be uncertainty as to whether and when they might go ahead. But without completing all eight projects, the strategic objectives for the corridor would be hard to deliver, the NAO concluded.

Perhaps anticipating criticism from the NAO, the Department for Transport commissioned a study of appraisal at programme level (Arup 2019). This addressed the problem of interdependence: how individual schemes might be complementary, competitive or independent of one another, such that the whole may be greater or less than the sum of the parts. The problem relates to investment in both corridors and regions, with no simple solutions since where both interdependencies and uncertainties exist, there is no longer a unique value for the expected benefit of any scheme.

The main conclusions of the study were that interdependency benefits could be material and programmatic analysis is complex, yet nevertheless, decision makers should have sight of a programmatic appraisal if the scheme they are making a decision about is materially related to other schemes. However, thus far the conclusions of this study appear to be too difficult to implement, although they are relevant to the formulation of a strategic-level context for transport investment, discussed below (see section 4.17).

Further examples of problematic road investment – in motorway widening – will be discussed in the next chapter (see section 5.4.1).

4.16.3 Airport investments

UK airports are for the most part in the private sector, so decisions to invest in new runway or terminal capacity are based on commercial considerations – principally increased returns to owners. Nevertheless, increasing airport capacity can have a significant environmental impact (an externality) so public scrutiny is warranted. Heathrow airport is the UK's largest, located relatively close to the centre of London, so that aircraft noise and surface traffic have always been a concern. Accordingly, a proposal by the airport to build a third runway prompted the UK government to set up an independent Airports Commission to consider the options for increasing capacity at Heathrow (it was implicit in the terms of reference that increased capacity would be needed). The Commission's report included economic analysis of options for the location of a third runway at the airport, as well as a further runway at Gatwick airport (Airports Commission 2015).

The Commission applied the DfT's standard approach to economic analysis, focusing on user benefits – the benefits to passengers – such as more frequent services made possible by increased capacity, and also lower fares resulting from more competition between airlines. To these, wider economic benefits were added, including from estimates of agglomeration effects. The outcome of the analysis depended on how carbon emission constraints might affect the economic case (an open policy question). To illustrate the main findings for the preferred runway option: benefits to users were estimated to be £55 billion present value from lower fares and greater frequencies; £11 billion from wider impacts; and £1 billion from reduced delays (Airports Commission 2015, Table 7.1). These estimates were crucially dependent on the supposition that increased capacity would result in increased competition that in turn would drive down fares.

The Commission's estimates of user benefits included those accruing to non-UK residents and to international travellers who simply change planes at Heathrow. However, the official guidance is that the impacts on non-UK residents should be excluded where it is possible to do so (TAG A5.2, 2022), which it should have been for a major study of the kind carried out. It has been argued that the exclusion of international passengers changing planes, who might amount to a majority of the additional passengers arising from a third runway, would result in a negative overall benefit (New Economics Foundation 2018).

One shortcoming of the approach of both the Airports Commission and the DfT has been to take as a given the need for additional airport capacity. It is assumed that more flights would promote exporting UK businesses, facilitated by more direct flights to far-flung markets; inward investment to Britain; and London as a world city for doing business. Arguably, there is little case for boosting tourism, given that outbound British travellers spend twice as much as inbound tourists. However, business travellers are only a minority of air passengers; even at Heathrow only a quarter of passengers are on business trips. If demand for business travel were to grow (and this has been made uncertain by the impact of the coronavirus pandemic), this would displace leisure travellers from Heathrow to other airports with spare capacity (Stansted and Luton in the London area; Birmingham accessed by HS2) through market forces, since business users would be willing to pay a premium for the attractions of Heathrow. As other airports approached capacity, fares would tend to rise, which would limit the most marginal leisure flying, for instance weekend city breaks for stag and hen parties, for which alternative UK destinations would allow more of the budget to be devoted to partying.

This failure to consider the wider airport system, and the requirements of different classes of user, illustrates the problem arising from a focus on the economic case for investment in a particular project. It contrasts with the case for HS2, where the specific project has been seen as meeting a need to increase capacity constraints in North–South rail links in England, and the supporting analysis estimated its impact on other rail routes. More generally, the case for particular investments needs to be set in a strategic context, as discussed next.

4.17 Strategic case for transport investment

The discussion thus far has been concerned with the economic justification of investments (or other interventions) as individual projects intended to improve the transport system. The economic case forms part of a wider process adopted by the UK Department for Transport for developing the business case for investments (DfT 2022a). This is consistent with the guidance issued by HM Treasury in the most recent edition of its Green Book (HMT 2022). There are five dimensions to the model, the commercial and management cases being not inherently controversial and largely beyond the scope of this book:

- the *strategic case* demonstrates how the proposal has a strong strategic fit to the organisation's priorities, government ambitions and the areas in scope;
- the *economic case* demonstrates the value for money and the best choice for maximising social welfare through options appraisal;
- the *commercial case* illustrates the commercial viability and supply-side capacity for the proposal;
- the *financial case* demonstrates the proposal is financially affordable;
- the *management case* sets out the proposal's deliverability through the effective development of plans, management and resources to oversee the project.

Setting out a strategic case for programmes of transport investments has been problematic, in part because transport is a derived demand – derived from people's need for access to destinations offering employment, services, activities, opportunities and choices. The investment case must therefore take into account how destinations would benefit from improved transport provision, which requires consideration of matters extending beyond the normal scope of transport investment appraisal. At project level, this issue has been side-stepped by the focus on travel time savings as a proxy for other benefits, but at strategic level, such an approach is less convincing.

In practice, the strategic case for programmes of transport investment has been set out in broad-brush terms. Consider the DfT's Road Investment Strategy, comprising five-year programmes of expenditure to maintain and develop England's Strategic Road Network, encompassing the motorways and major roads. The objectives for a third such programme for the period 2025–30, known as RIS3, have been issued for consultation (DfT 2021c). These objectives have been couched in very general terms – improving safety, network performance, environmental outcomes, growing the economy. There is no economic content to the strategy, which therefore lacks a rationale for what is expected to be a very large expenditure programme (the current RIS2 programme was worth £27 billion when announced).

In early 2023 the DfT issued a draft National Networks Policy Statement covering road and rail infrastructure, intended to preclude local public inquiries into proposed schemes from considering matters of national policy. However, this statement essentially deals with procedural aspects relevant to proposals for individual schemes, and does not make a case for a strategic approach to justify programmes of investment.

In late 2023 the DfT issued a new TAG unit on the topic of Spending Objective Analysis, with the aim of promoting alignment between the economic and strategic dimensions of transport business cases. The intention is to allow understanding of the composition of the benefits and costs that contribute to the benefit–cost ratio and how they link to the objectives of the proposed scheme, for instance how they support the economic development of a specific locality. However, this approach is concerned with the strategic aspects of individual investments, not with programmes of investments for which strategic thinking is most needed. This limits its usefulness while making more complex the appraisal process.

The Welsh government, which has devolved responsibility for transport, initiated a review of roads investment prompted by the need to reduce carbon emissions and the number of journeys made by car. The outcome of this review reflects a very different strategic perspective to that adopted in England, with a focus on minimising carbon emissions, not increasing road capacity, and not increasing emissions through higher vehicle speeds (discussed further in the next section). However, there is no economic content to this strategic perspective.

It would be desirable to incorporate economic analysis into the strategic case for a programme of investments. However, this cannot simply involve aggregating the predominantly time saving benefits expected from the individual schemes on account of the issues of complementarity and competition, discussed in the context of the A303 case (see section 4.16.2). Moreover, the strategic case for a major transport investment is likely to reflect the potential of the wider impacts (see section 4.9), but taking such impacts separately from conventional transport user benefits would not generally be of sufficient magnitude in aggregate to provide adequate justification.

The National Infrastructure Commission developed a multi-criteria assessment that included valuation of the economic benefits of rail improvements that allowed an increase in the density of cities, and thence of agglomeration benefits for both businesses and consumers (NIC 2020). Although this was not fully articulated, it has promise for more general application, given the intention to include all significant benefits. The Commission also investigated a general methodology for estimating the uplift in real estate values arising from transport investment (see section 4.10). There are also the specific cases of the Northern Line Extension and river crossings in East London, where changes in land use and value were estimated to support the investment decision (see section 4.10). Uplift in observable real estate values is a more convincing proxy for the economic benefits of transport investment than notional travel time savings and would be applicable at programme level and hence to making a strategic case.

The main benefit of transport investment is improved access. In principle, it would be desirable to value such improvements. However, as discussed previously, attributing values to access has not proved feasible in practice (see section 4.12). In particular, the value of access is subject to diminishing returns, at a rate that depends on the type of destination, which makes quantification difficult.

Another approach to including economic content in the strategic case would be to employ cost-effectiveness analysis, to provide context for the cost–benefit approach of the economic case. One example of cost-effectiveness analysis is the use of the marginal abatement cost (MAC) to set the value of carbon used in investment appraisal (DBEIS 2021). This involves estimating the unit cost (£ per tonne of CO_2 equivalent, or £/tCO2e) of carbon abatement delivered by the whole range of relevant technologies, including transport technologies. These are then ranked graphically in order of cost, the width of each block of the histogram reflecting the contribution expected from each technology (some technologies, such as building insulation, can pay for themselves through energy cost saving, so have negative carbon values). The level of emission reduction to meet the national target can be read off, together with the corresponding carbon value.

Wider application of the MAC approach could be considered, replacing carbon costs by the value of other desired outcomes. The problem then is to devise a single criterion with a monetised value. The MAC approach could be used to prioritise transport investments in terms of meeting carbon reduction objectives for the sector, but this would disregard other transport policy objectives. In general, transport investments have multiple objectives, and the focus on time savings as the main benefit has been counterproductive, as discussed in this chapter.

Where an approach to assessing cost-effectiveness at strategic level might be useful would be for a regional body with a devolved budget to rank interventions in order of effectiveness in meeting policy priorities, as these are seen in the region. How transport investments in the various modes and locations ranked in relation to other kinds of investment could well be substantially different from existing priorities determined largely by provisions of funds from the various central government departments. Investment, for instance, in fast broadband digital connectivity or electric charging points for electric vehicles could be judged more important than a road scheme intended (but failing) to lessen congestion.

A further economic function for the strategic case would be to articulate the expected contribution of a programme of transport investments to improved economic performance. This would depend on the ability to quantify such contributions, which in principle could be estimated and modelled, but in practice such modelling involves great complexity and uncertainty and is therefore contentious.

The strategic rationale for transport investment will be further considered later in this book, in the context of countering climate change. It will be argued that the importance of decarbonisation is such that this consideration should provide the predominant strategic framework for future transport investments and policies.

4.18 Governance

The practice of transport investment appraisal is embedded in a governance framework that influences the application of economic theory and which varies between countries. As Baldwin and Shuttleworth (2021) observe, the UK has a particularly large and powerful central ministry in the DfT, which holds most of the functions that generate and analyse evidence, but is weak in respect of external scrutiny of evidence underlying decisions. External scrutiny is discouraged by the failure to publish the traffic and economic modelling studies that are the basis for the business cases for proposed investments. Businesses cases themselves are published exceptionally, not routinely. The National Audit Office has issued critical analyses of transport investments, for instance the A303 Stonehenge scheme (see section 4.15.2), but its coverage of transport is limited, given that its remit is to examine value for money across public expenditure as a whole.

The Department's Transport Analysis Guidance (TAG), amounting to over 1,000 pages plus accompanying spreadsheets and computer programmes, is effectively accessible only to specialists, who earn their living by the practice of their expertise and so do not challenge the prescribed approach. In this respect the transport sector is anomalous in that in most areas of British professional life, the professions themselves lead in setting the standards and methodologies. The existence of a single body responsible both for providing the vast bulk of public funds for transport investment and for prescribing the methodology for investment appraisal is not conducive to fresh thinking about solutions to the problems faced by the sector, not least reducing its contribution to global warming.

Wales has substantial devolved responsibility for transport and is able to follow a distinct policy path. The Welsh government has promulgated its own guidance, known as WelTAG, which broadly follows the TAG approach to estimating value for money, with one important difference (WelTAG 2022). There is some ambivalence about calculating benefit–cost ratios, regarded as not proportionate for smaller projects but necessary for those requiring funding from the UK government. Where larger projects rely on funding from the Welsh government, two sets of benefit–cost ratios will be needed – one that includes travel time savings as a benefit, and a second that excludes such benefits. Monetised time savings are to be separated out to show the distribution of time savings (for example 0–2 minutes, 2–5 minutes and 5 minutes plus), to enable decision makers to see the impacts and the distribution of benefits separately and aid in making judgements on the impact of the time savings in achieving policy objectives.

This treatment of travel time savings reflects the Welsh government's policy objective to improve journey times for active travel and public transport, to make them time-competitive against the private car and encourage a shift to more sustainable modes of travel. Taking into account travel time savings for car drivers would encourage more car use, and would run counter to legislation to restrict speeds on most local roads to 20 mph.[3] However, the disregard of user benefits in the form of time savings, without their replacement, means that economic analysis is effectively omitted, hence the change in terminology, replacing the 'economic case' by a 'well-being case'. What we then have is what Hickman and Dean (2018) term 'participatory multi-criteria analysis', with the BCR as just one criterion among many or omitted altogether. However, investment appraisal without economic content seems like an oxymoron. What is missing is a methodology that values the benefits of an intervention to all classes of traveller, to help judge to what extent the intended mode shift would yield a net benefit in magnitude and better distribution. An approach based on valuing access benefits could in principle be attractive, offsetting loss of access to private car users by gains of access to those using active travel or public transport. Yet, as noted in section 4.12, methodology for attributing monetary values to access improvements has not been developed.

Scotland also has devolved responsibility for transport. The Scottish government's guidance follows the DfT's guidance, including standard cost–benefit analysis focused on user benefits plus wider economic impacts (STAG 2022).

The UK's approach to transport investment is characterised by government departments both providing the funds and prescribing the appraisal methodology at length in fine detail. While there is a logic to this as a means of ensuring value for money is achieved for public expenditure, it contributes to thinking within a silo on the part of officials and the consultants from whom advice is sought. Development of the methodology is incremental, adding further features as these achieve policy prominence, but not asking what is going on in practice – hence, for instance, nugatory expenditure on futile attempts to reduce congestion. Fresh thinking is not encouraged.

In other sectors of the economy, professional standards and methodological good practice are set by the professions, allowing scope for debate and development. However, the professions of transport economists and transport planners are not offering persuasive thought leadership, regrettably.

4.19 Economics of competition

The discussion in this chapter thus far has focused on the problems arising from the conventional economic analysis of transport investments. Economic analysis has also been applied to the provision of public transport services in the context of the political debate about whether monopolistic providers should be broken up and exposed to competition, a feature of the emergence of the neoliberal political perspective of the late twentieth century. Some aspects of this discussion are briefly summarised below.

In Britain, most bus services were run by local authorities after the Second World War, and rail services were operated by a state-owned corporation, British Rail. The Thatcher government of the 1980s very largely privatised bus services outside London, permitting on-street competition between operators. The rail industry was also privatised, separating ownership of infrastructure and operations, with competitive bidding by private-sector operators for franchises of specified periods to run the trains on specified routes. In the US, airline deregulation resulted in the restructuring of the industry, with many low-cost operators entering the market and some well-known brands departing – illustrating the potential of changes in governance to deliver benefits to users.

Privatisation and deregulation policies were influenced by economists who believed in the benefits of competition and were critical of monopolistic public ownership. A regular series of international conferences focused on competition in land passenger transport, known as the Thredbo series, after the Australian resort where the first meeting was held in 1989 (Wong and Hensher 2018). The limits of on-road competition of buses were recognised, given the tendency of passengers to board the first available bus, which meant the operators had no incentive to compete on price. Predatory behaviour by operators was also recognised, sacrificing part of their profit after entry of a competitor, with the aim of driving them out and deterring others.

In recent years there has been a shift of political opinion away from a focus on the benefits of competition in public transport provision, the consequence of a variety of market failures. Hence in Britain the rail industry is being returned to the responsibility of a state-owned public body, known as Great British Railways, which will operate the rail infrastructure and also control the contracting of passenger train services, the setting of fares and timetables and the collection of fare revenue. For buses, the direction of policy is to move generally towards the arrangements that have been successful in London, where the public body, Transport for London, is responsible for a fully integrated service, with multimodal tickets, bus priority measures, high-quality information for passengers, turn-up-and-go frequencies and services that keep running into the evenings and at weekends. Worsley and Mackie (2015) have argued that policy on rail and bus organisation policy tends to be formed through some more or less ideological prism, and analysis is used in a subordinate role to provide support for a predetermined direction of travel and to help inform key policy choices within the mission. White (2018) has provided an account of recent bus industry developments in Britain, and Preston (2023) has discussed both bus and rail industry developments.

The focus by the economists on the efficiency benefits of competition for public transport led to practical and theoretical debate about how to administer subsidy for routes that would not be commercially viable but were judged socially desirable, and how to regulate the sector in a way that protected the consumer while fostering competition. Yet little attention was paid to the economic benefits of integration of services across the modes of travel, which can be of great value to users in practice, albeit difficult to value in theory, one example of the limitations of economic analysis.

4.20 Limits of economic analysis

The discussion in this chapter has largely focused on the problems arising from the conventional economic analysis of transport investments. There are, as well, problematic aspects of economic analysis generally, which are now briefly discussed.

Progress in the physical sciences has depended on the mathematical formulation of the behaviour of the entities studied, from subatomic particles to galaxies. Comparison of theory against observation allows theories to be tested rigorously. A trend in economics since the middle of the last century has involved the mathematical formulation of the behaviour of economic agents, humans and businesses, a tendency sometimes criticised as motivated by 'physics envy'. A substantial body of economic theory has been developed in which consumers are represented as optimising their utility in full knowledge of the options, subject to budget constraints on both time and money. However, such mathematical formalisation generally requires behavioural simplification for modelling to be tractable.

Thaler (2000) distinguished between normative and descriptive theories in economics. The former are characterised by rational choice involving maximisation of expected utility, the latter by the attempt to characterise actual choices based on observed behaviour. With the application of mathematical formulations of economic behaviour, economic agents have become more explicitly optimising. However, Thaler suggests that in the future this 'homo economicus' will evolve so that economic models incorporate more realistic conceptions of human cognition and emotions – the basis of the sub-discipline of behavioural economics, which identifies a considerable diversity of factors that are likely to explain systematic deviations of human behaviour from the predictions of rational models. As yet, application to transport analysis remains quite limited (see for example Metcalf and Dolan 2012; Avineri 2012).

The orthodox approach to transport economic analysis is essentially normative, based on a simplifying assumption, paradigm or 'stylised fact', that interventions that permit faster travel result in users saving time, time that can be valued by engaging users in experiments that trade off travel time and travel cost. In contrast, the approach suggested by this book's critique would be based on observed behaviour, notably that the benefits of faster travel are taken as improved access, which would be a better basis for policy and investment decisions.

4.21 Conclusions

Cost–benefit appraisal of transport investments has been developed in the UK over the past 60 years, based on an orthodox microeconomic framework in which the saving of travel time has constituted the preponderant economic benefit, as outlined in an instructive account by Worsley and Mackie (2015), who also recognise its limitations. A number of other countries have adopted a broadly similar approach (Mackie, Worsley and Eliasson 2014). The methodology was originally developed to help decision makers choose between a large number of road-based options, which justified a simplistic analysis, including importantly the assumption that new capacity did not result in an increase in traffic (known as the 'fixed trip matrix assumption'). However, in subsequent years, the aims of transport investment have been extended to encompass other modes of travel and a range of objectives relating to economic growth, employment, quality of life and environmental outcomes. These further objectives were incorporated into the economic analysis both by recognising, at least in principle, the reality of induced traffic arising from new capacity and the associated increase in value of externalities, and by bolting on estimates of wider impacts, such as agglomeration benefits, to the pre-existing microeconomic framework.

In essence, what has evolved is a core analysis based substantially on the value of travel time savings to users, tacitly assuming origins and destinations are fixed, but recognising that exogenous factors will vary – demographic, income, car ownership, energy prices and others. To this is added the value of the economic consequences that arise because a reduction in the cost of travel results in wider economic impacts, not encompassed by user benefits, with both positive benefits and negative externalities. The limitations of this approach are generally recognised by its proponents (see, for instance, Mackie, Worsley and Eliasson 2014). Nevertheless, it is noteworthy that a comprehensive methodology has not yet been settled, even after more than half a century of effort. The difficulties with the orthodox approach, discussed in this chapter, may be summarised as follows.

First, while the main benefit from transport investment is conventionally taken as the saving of travel time, a number of problems arise when estimating the monetary value of travel time savings:

- Values based on stated preference (SP) experiments reflect respondents' short-run preferences, whereas investments yield long-term benefits.
- It has proved difficult to validate SP estimates by reference to observed travel behaviour.
- Value of time estimates vary depending on context – whether gains or losses, and their magnitude.

- Time savings in practice are typically quite small; small time savings are found to have lower unit values than larger savings.
- The economic theory that is the basis of appraisal excludes the behavioural effects that are required to explain the responses to SP surveys.
- Valuing reliability and comfort has been carried out as part of the SP surveys focused on travel time savings, yet improving reliability and comfort can be achieved in the absence of time savings and so should be valued independently.

Besides these problems associated with estimating the unit value of travel time savings, there also major issues with the conventional approach to transport investment appraisal that focuses on estimating the magnitude of time savings:

- Although the main benefit from transport investment is conventionally taken as the saving of travel time, this is inconsistent with the long-run invariance of average travel time observed in population surveys of travel behaviour. Investment that makes possible faster travel allows greater access to desired destinations, to more people, places, activities and services, thus enhancing opportunities and choices. The main benefits of investment are therefore access benefits. It is accordingly inappropriate to treat time savings as one element of 'generalised costs', for the purpose if microeconomic analysis.
- Greater access achieved by road travel results in more traffic, known as induced traffic, which in turn leads to increased externalities related to vehicle-miles travelled, including carbon and pollutant emissions, and increased congestion.
- Road traffic congestion is common in or near densely populated urban areas with high levels of car ownership. It is largely self-regulating, in that as traffic increases, so do delays, which prompt some potential road users to make other choices. For the same reason, attempts to mitigate congestion fail, whether by increasing road capacity or promoting other modes of travel, since reduced delays attract back previously suppressed trips.
- Road pricing is seen by economists as the best way to reduce congestion, but the cost of inequity, as experienced by low-income road users priced off the network, is not taken into account, a likely reason why road pricing has rarely been adopted.

- Beyond the conventional user benefits from transport improvements, conceptually there are wider economic impacts, some arising from better connectivity for a given spatial distribution of economic activity, and some that occur as transport improvements change the pattern of private-sector investment. Estimating the value of agglomeration and other wider impacts is challenging and prone to optimism bias. Besides, conventional user benefits, which are the foundation upon which the wider impacts are based, are derived from survey respondents' short-term preferences, whose relationship to long-run economic benefits is tenuous.
- Changes in land use and value are a general consequence of transport investment but are not central to conventional transport economic appraisal, for which notional time savings are regarded as the main benefit, rather than the real-world consequences.
- The main benefit from transport investment is better access – to people and destinations for employment, activities and services – with the ensuing increase in opportunities and choices. However, access measures have proved difficult to quantify and monetise for appraisal purposes.
- As the speed of travel increases, access increases, but because access is subject to diminishing returns, the growth of demand for travel slows then ceases. The resulting travel demand saturation means that transport investment is subject to diminishing returns.
- Populations are diverse, yet transport investment appraisal in practice is able to reflect only one part of this diversity in monetary terms – the variation of the value of travel time saving by income class. Other aspects are treated qualitatively.
- Transport investment has consequences for those other than users of the transport system, mostly as costs borne by others, known as externalities. Some can be given monetary values, allowing these to be taken into account in cost–benefit analysis – including air pollution, carbon emissions and casualties from collisions. Others are treated only qualitatively.
- The health benefits of active travel can be monetised and incorporated into cost–benefit analysis of proposed cycle improvements, but the wider implication for road use may not be fully recognised.
- Investments benefits are usually estimated over a 60-year period from opening, although 100 years is not precluded and would yield larger benefits. Uncertainties increase over time, for both the with- and without-investment cases.

Consideration of a number of well-documented case studies of transport investments draws attention to further problems with conventional cost–benefit analysis:

- The lack of indication of spatial distribution of economic benefits.
- The inconsistency between appraisal, based on notional time savings and inferred wider economic impacts, and evaluation that addresses real observable outcomes of investments.
- Conventional estimation of economic benefits of an investment that is politically salient may be insufficient to achieve an acceptable value for money rating. This may prompt ad hoc recourse to alternative methodologies to achieve the desired investment decision.
- The economic benefits of an individual investment may depend on the impact of other investments along a route or within a region. There is a lack of a general methodology to address such interactions, as well as to place individual investments in a strategic economic context.

These problems associated with the conventional transport economic appraisal methodology are exacerbated in the UK because the DfT is both prescriber of the methodology and the dominant source of public funding for the sector, considerations that are not receptive to critical analysis nor conducive to fresh thinking.

Notwithstanding these many issues, cost–benefit analysis can be seen as a way of providing some economic discipline to the allocation of scarce public resources, both between the competing projects of an investment programme and between such programmes. So, despite the problems with the current approach to appraisal, we need to address whether there are alternative approaches better suited to the problems of the twenty-first century, as will be discussed in Chapter 7.

The next chapter is concerned with transport modelling, which is the means by which the expected consequences of investment decisions are translated into monetary values for economic analysis.

Notes

1   These values, rounded, are taken from the Department for Transport's TAG Data Book Table A1.3.1, May 2022. The values are for the year 2010, at market prices.
2   Rounded values (2010 prices), taken from TAG Data Book Table A4.1.1, May 2022.
3   Implemented by means of the Restricted Roads (20 mph Speed Limit) (Wales) Order 2022.

5
Transport models reconsidered

5.1 Introduction

Economic analysis of proposed interventions to improve the transport system requires the modelling of the expected outcomes and of the situation that would arise without the intervention. These are sometimes referred to as the 'do something' and 'do nothing' (or 'do minimum') cases, or the 'with-investment' and 'without-investment' cases. To make the comparison, models of the transport system have been developed that are intended to project travel behaviour into the future, in particular to project travel times, given that the main benefit of investment is supposed to be the saving of travel time.

Transport models, which might also be called travel models, are complex and opaque, and are based on limited data, with many numerical parameters whose magnitude may require expert judgement in their specification. Accordingly, a distinction may be made between 'experts' and 'non-experts' in respect of a working understanding of transport models. Experts will generally earn their living as professional transport modellers and naturally have an interest in both justifying and advancing practice. Non-experts vary in their interest. Many are content to accept the outcome of modelling as provided, particularly if it conforms to prior expectation, for instance that a project forming part of an investment programme is forecast to offer good value for money. Others, notably those who are critical of particular schemes, would like to understand better the modelling that supports the proposed investment ahead of a public inquiry, but find it difficult to penetrate the published documentation, which, in any case, is only a report of the outcome of the detailed analysis, not the analysis itself. They see transport models as 'black boxes', whose workings are not visible to scrutiny.

The perspective from which this chapter is written is that of a non-expert with a close interest in transport models and their applications – a view from the outside, so to speak. We start with an outline of the most commonly used type of transport model and go on to discuss evidence relevant to the validity of such models in forecasting future travel behaviour, following which other approaches to modelling will be considered.

As well as references cited below, there are two comprehensive volumes on the topic of transport modelling: the mathematically detailed standard text of Ortuzar and Willumsen (2011) in its fourth edition, and the historical, non-mathematical approach to the modelling of urban travel demand of Boyce and Williams (2015). The UK Department for Transport (DfT) has issued a number of units devoted to modelling in its Transport Analysis Guidance, cited below as 'TAG Unit MXX, date', as in the previous chapter; these are fairly prescriptive for schemes requiring public funding. Transport for London has published an outline guide to the strategic models it uses (TfL n.d.) as well as a detailed account of its approach to traffic modelling (TfL 2021a). Yaron Hollander's self-published *Transport Modelling for a Complete Beginner* provides a readable and informative outline (Hollander 2016). He is a rare, probably unique, example of an expert who has departed the field, leaving a critical study as a legacy.

5.2 Four stage models

The classic structure for a transport model involves four stages, briefly outlined below as the basis for consideration of the features of the generality of transport models. It is assumed that travel behaviour reflects the sequential choices made by individuals at each of the following stages:

- Trip generation, which involves estimation of the number of trips to and from each geographical zone of the study area, for each demand segment defined by journey purpose, person type, car availability, etc.;
- Mode split – how the estimated trips divide between the available modes of travel;
- Trip distribution – each trip is linked to an origin and destination;
- Trip assignment, in which routes through the network are allocated between origins and destinations. This involves minimising the generalised costs of travel (see section 4.2).

A model is calibrated with observed or inferred data for a specific point in time, the 'base year', using a cross-sectional data set. The reason to construct a model is to estimate the consequences for future travel behaviour of external changes, whether the result of interventions such as an investment in the transport system, or changes in the wider economy, such as income growth. Such external changes are inputted into the model to yield projections of matters of interest, whether operational, such as the level of congestion on particular roads, or more broadly, particularly to estimate the economic benefits, comparing with- and without-investment cases. For this purpose, assumptions must be made about how changes in external factors lead to changes in model parameters. However, relationships may vary over time, which means that the calibration of models intended for forecasting should be checked by comparing prediction with outcome using longitudinal data.

A major concern of modellers is to fit observed behaviour to an established analytical framework, for which purpose it is necessary to cope with limited data availability and to make simplifying behavioural assumptions, in the interests of computability. There is an assumption that individuals belong to a homogeneous sub-population, who act rationally and make choices that maximise their net personal utility, subject to a variety of constraints. However, the modeller has incomplete access to the motivation of individuals and so must make assumptions about the range of possible behaviours (as in so-called 'random utility' models).

The outcome of modelling in practice depends on the features of the model, including what simplifications are made to reduce data and computing requirements. Simplifications can include:

- keeping the total number of trips fixed, or keeping the origins and destinations fixed. However, in reality, an investment that reduces the cost of travel would lead to more trips being made, including to new destinations;
- the level of disaggregation of zones of origin and destination;
- assuming that past relationships between the parameters used in the model will continue to apply in the future. Yet as discussed previously, there is evidence of breaks in trends in travel behaviour (see section 2.2);
- assuming a particular hierarchy of decisions. In the four stages outlined above, mode split is above trip distribution, reflecting UK evidence suggesting a preference for a specific mode before a destination is chosen (TAG M2.1, 4.5, 2024). However, in other situations, distribution may be ranked above mode, for instance for home-to-work trips in circumstances where alternative modes are available;

- assuming that land use does not change as a result of a transport investment, disregarding the possibility that the location of businesses might change as a result of improved transport provision;
- making simplifying assumptions about how road users perceive the monetary costs of travel, fuel costs and tolls;
- making simplifying assumptions about what knowledge travellers have of alternative routes and modes of travel, and of the travel times involved. Ortuzar and Willumsen (2011, 411) observe that the usual (unrealistic) assumptions made by modellers are that the traveller has full knowledge of generalised costs of every route; delays on a link are due only to flows on that link; and demand and flows over a modelled period do not change over time.
- disregarding how people may shift their times and routes of travel to avoid congestion or crowding at times of peak use of transport networks;
- disregarding how people may make a chain of trips that start and end at the same place, usually home;
- disregarding the need for parking at both ends of a trip if the car is to be the preferred travel mode.

All the above simplifications can be replaced by more elaborate treatments to achieve more realistic representations of travel behaviour. Whether this is justified has depended on the professional judgement of modellers in the light of client requirements and resources available. The case for making simplifications is to illuminate the most important underlying relationships, but any simplification must ultimately be judged by testing model validity, by comparing forecast with observed outturn.

5.3 Model validation

Some model parameters can be observed directly, for instance the structure of the network or the composition of traffic. Others have to be inferred indirectly, such as choice of travel modes as this is influenced by quality attributes. Appropriate choice of parameters aims to reflect behaviours implicit in a simplified theory of how the system works. Because most parameters have to be inferred, the calibration process involves guessing such values, then running the model and comparing modelled outcomes with real-world observed outcomes, such as travel times or traffic volumes for the base year. This is done repeatedly (iteratively) until a good match between model output and observation is achieved (known as convergence).

It is the practice for calibration to use only part of the available data. In what is termed 'model validation', the model is run to see if it can estimate what is in the other part – that is, the base year data not used for calibration. Data might be split randomly or by geography. However, as Hollander (2016, 77) notes, if some traffic phenomena or travel behaviours are not evident in the calibration data, they may often be missing from the validation data as well, which could lead to overconfidence in the model's performance.

Model validation, as practised by transport modellers, is essentially a cross-check on the calibration. More generally, however, the concept of validation of any kind of model involves comparing forecast with outcome, with good correspondence increasing confidence in both the model and the underlying theory. Such predictive validation is most rigorous in the physical sciences, where small discrepancies between prediction and observation may necessitate adjustment to, or even replacement of, the theory. Even in a field as complex as weather forecasting, substantial advances have been made in recent years through the accumulation of scientific knowledge and advances in computing, comparing prediction with observation (Bauer, Thorpe and Brunet 2015).

For small-scale transport models, as may be used to reproduce the behaviour of traffic in a neighbourhood prior to making an intervention such as changing the timing of traffic signals, observed outcomes can be fed back to refine the model calibration for future use. However, this gets progressively more difficult as the area of interest enlarges to the town, city, region and country, as other modes of travel are included, and as the timescale extends to cover the life of an investment.

The factors that might result in mismatch between model forecast and observed outturn include: projections of exogenous inputs differing from assumption, for instance income and population growth, energy prices and technological innovation; misspecification of the model; errors in model parameters as estimated; and data shortcomings. These possibilities will be discussed below. The main point is that unless comparison of forecast with outturn can be used diagnostically to improve the performance of a model in subsequent applications, the use of the model as an aid to making decisions about investments or other interventions must be of uncertain predictive validity.

A general problem in model construction and calibration is the tendency of those involved to be overly optimistic about key parameters, which may lead to discrepancy between forecast and outturn. Given the judgements about model parameters and structures that must be made to achieve outputs that would appear credible to the clients who commission modelling, there is inevitably scope for bias on the part of the modellers, whether conscious or unconscious, within the bounds of professional respectability. This depends in part on the political and organisational context in which models are used to inform decisions on transport investments (Hollander 2016, 220). In the public sector, models may be used to set priorities within a programme of investment, to justify individual projects as good value for money and to decide between projects competing for limited funds. In the private sector, models may be used to help decide whether to participate in a commercial activity. It is therefore commonly the case that those commissioning modelling will have a prior expectation of the outcome, for instance that a project forming part of a programme for which funding has been allocated would offer good value for money, or that a bid would be competitive in relation to other proposals. Moreover, because the effort required to build a model is considerable, resources may not be made available until there is substantial interest in the proposed investment, such that choice between options has already been made, in which case there is pressure on the modellers to justify prior decisions. All these considerations may lead to optimism bias of one kind or another, which is not generally countered by evaluation of outcomes, on account of both the lapse of time and the lack of granularity of outcome-monitoring exercises. Nevertheless, there are cases where forecast and outcome have been compared, with illuminating results.

Estimates of the capital costs of an investment are important for economic appraisal with focus on the benefit–cost ratio. To allow for optimism bias, the DfT recommends uplifts to capital cost estimates that depend on the type and stage of development of a project; for instance, for roads, uplifts of 46 per cent at the earliest stage of planning, declining to 20 per cent prior to construction (TAG A1.2, 3.5.8, 2022). Errors in forecasting capital costs become apparent on completion of construction and can be used to improve future such forecasts by means of the Reference Class Forecasting methodology (Flyvbjerg 2008; Oxford Global Projects 2020).

Errors in estimating future demand are evident from observed outturn usage, but it is more difficult to identify the underlying causes and feed these back into model improvement, in part because of lack of granularity of the observed data. Evaluation of the outcome of road investments is generally restricted to traffic counts at a limited number of time points after opening. There is an extensive literature on the accuracy of traffic forecasting for new highway construction. Erhardt et al. (2020) analysed a large database of forecast average daily traffic in comparison to observed traffic counts for the first post-opening year available, finding on average counted traffic volumes about 6 per cent lower than forecast. This study also looked in detail at six projects, finding diverse contributing factors to forecasting inaccuracy but in all cases identifying optimism bias in that forecast traffic was greater than observed traffic. Another review by Cruz and Sarmento (2019) confirms the importance of optimism bias. Optimism bias in forecasting has for some time been recognised in relation to transport investments, notably by Flyvbjerg (2007). Optimism bias in forecasting demand has been a particular concern for privately financed toll roads, where traffic and revenues may fall short of the expectations of investors, as documented by Bain (2009).

While the benefits of toll road construction are evident from the revenues and can be compared with the modelled forecasts, it is rare to find reports of whether the economic benefits of publicly financed roads are achieved in practice. Travel time savings seem less commonly reported, even though they are supposed to be the main contributing element of the economic benefits of public investment.

5.4 Model performance

A review of the outcome of transport investments noted that while one of the purposes of ex-post evaluation would be to test the predictive validity of the transport model, this is infrequent for a variety of reasons (Worsley 2015). There are, nevertheless, some revealing case studies, discussed next.

5.4.1 Modelling road investments

There has been an investment programme to add capacity to England's motorways by converting the hard shoulder to a running lane, typically from three to four lanes in each direction, with variable message signs to regulate flows; these are known as 'smart motorways'. Data has become available that enables comparison in certain cases of forecast with outturn traffic flows, both volume and speed. In the case of the scheme on the M25 London orbital route between junctions 23 and 27, to the north of the city centre, monitoring reports were available for before the scheme opened and for three successive years after opening. While the traffic flowed faster at year one after opening, there was a noteworthy absence of journey time reduction at years two and three, compared with before – not what had been predicted by the modelling (Metz 2021b).

The forecasting of how the traffic flows would change, comparing the with- and without-investment cases, employed the long-established SATURN variable demand network model (Hall, Van Vliet and Willumsen 1980; Boyce and Williams 2015, 411–13). This has been maintained and developed by a leading transport consultant under the oversight of the originator and is recognised as consistent with the requirements of the

UK DfT that the effects of variable demand on scheme benefits should be estimated quantitatively. As with all such transport models that are employed to inform investment decisions, a key output is changes in journey time that result from the intended investment, as input to the calculation of economic benefit, for which purpose the DfT's Transport User Benefit Appraisal (TUBA) software was employed.

The main forecast economic benefits were projected to be the value of time savings to business users. There were also time savings to non-business users, commuters and others, but these were entirely offset by increased vehicle operating costs, consistent with local users diverting to take advantage of the shorter journey times made possible by the increased road capacity on the motorway. Based on these forecasts, the benefit–cost ratio prior to the decision to construct was 2.9. However, in light of the observed absence of travel time savings beyond year one, it is likely that diversion by local users was underestimated by the model, with a likely contribution arising from the impact of widely used digital navigation (generally known as satnav), which makes evident the fastest routes to local users who are able to exercise choice.

So, in this M25 widening case, there was a substantial discrepancy between model forecast and outturn as early as year two after opening. A second such example involves a similar widening of the M1 motorway between junctions 10 and 13 to the north of London. Evaluation five years after opening found that the traffic moved more slowly than before the scheme opened, contrary to expectation (Metz 2023b). Forecasts of traffic flows and economic benefits had been generated by SATURN and TUBA modelling. Substantial net benefits to business users were forecast, whereas for non-business users, time-saving benefits were more than offset by increased vehicle operation costs, consistent with diversion of local trips to take advantage of the increase in capacity. As before, such diversion is likely to be facilitated by the wide adoption by road users of digital navigation route guidance.

Estimation of values of travel time savings, discussed earlier (see section 4.5), found that values were 2.4- to 4-fold higher for road users experiencing heavily congested traffic compared with free flow, implying that users would be willing to travel significantly longer distances to avoid congested traffic (Batley, Dekker and Mackie 2022). This is consistent with users diverting to take advantage of new, less congested motorway capacity. A further analysis concluded that the use of congestion-dependent values of travel time in modelling would have a significant impact on forecast flows, with implications for options appraisal and scheme design, and would also have a significant impact on the economic appraisal of road schemes, with implications for investment decisions (WSP 2022).

The DfT has not yet adopted values of time that depend on congestion, preferring values that reflect average traffic conditions – a further example of a simplification used in modelling that has questionable validity. Using congestion-dependent values would increase the apparent economic benefits of road investment, since the main aim of such investment is to reduce congestion. However, higher values of time for congested conditions, estimated in willingness to pay experiments, reflect personal discomfort of road users, whereas had the previous methodology of valuing time for those travelling on employers' business still been used (based on labour market values of time lost from work), such personal discomfort would not be relevant. So it is perhaps not surprising that the DfT has been cautious in treating the level of congestion as a relevant variable for economic appraisal, even though its disregard is inappropriate for modelling purposes.

These two case studies of investment to increase highway capacity point up the failure of a long-established transport modelling framework to project traffic flows as early as two to five years after scheme opening. The two studies outlined above attract attention on account of marked discrepancy between outcome and forecast. In contrast, a meta-analysis of a variety of UK road investments that compared predicted and observed journey times savings found generally good agreement for most schemes, for which savings of less than 200 seconds were predicted, although with 65 per cent of the observed peak hour journey time savings less than predicted (Highways England 2016). This would suggest that the models performed well. However, evaluation that monitors only overall traffic volumes and average speeds lacks the granularity needed to distinguish between local users and long-distance business users, which is important since the economic case for investment in additional capacity depends on the time-saving benefits to the latter. Underlying an outcome that appears to align well with the forecast, local users might be taking (unobserved) a greater share of the new capacity, pre-empting capacity intended for business users, both cars and road freight. A report making recommendations as to how evaluation of outcomes could inform appraisal did not recognise this crucial distinction (DfT 2016b).

This superficiality of conventional ex-post evaluation contrasts with the ex-ante modelling of traffic, which recognises different classes of user having different values of time. It is possible to take advantage of vehicle tracking by providers of digital navigation services to distinguish between traffic that remains on a segment of motorway of interest from beginning to end, and that which enters and leaves within the segment, as illustrated by the analysis of traffic using the M25 by Gilmour and

Flynn (2020). This distinction would allow the improvement of the calibration of traffic models, which are commonly used repeatedly to appraise a variety of proposed investments within the region for which the model has been developed. It would also provide better estimates of the economic benefits of the investment.

5.4.2 Modelling long-term traffic growth

The UK DfT has been operating a National Transport Model (NTM) through a series of updates and upgrades for more than 20 years. It is a multimodal model of land-based transport in Great Britain, quite broad brush and at the same time quite elaborate, involving a number of bespoke components: a four-stage model of personal travel demand; freight and public transport models; a car ownership model; and inputs from the National Travel Survey, and from a national trip end model (NTEM) that takes account of changes in population, employment and housing (DfT 2020b). The main purpose is to provide national road traffic forecasts to inform road investment decisions.

Goodwin (2019, 159) has noted the tendency of British national forecasts of road traffic levels over a 25-year period to substantially overestimate actual traffic growth, and Levinson (2014) has documented other examples. The DfT has argued that the primary sources for these discrepancies were what turned out to be erroneous input assumptions about economic and population growth and fuel costs, based on the advice of other government departments, which affected travel demand (DfT 2018b). A 'backcast' exercise was attempted, in which the NTM, calibrated to 2015 data, was run 'in reverse' to project traffic in 2003, which could be compared with observed traffic in that year for a number of scenarios that reflected estimated of travel demand in the earlier year. Good agreement was claimed between backcast and actual traffic levels overall, although less so for London, where alternative modes to the car are more available than elsewhere. However, inspection of the account of the backcasting exercise (DfT 2020b, section 4) suggests considerable difficulty in extracting convincing conclusions. Moreover, a peer review of the performance of the model noted that the backcasting exercise was limited to only the demand and traffic assignment part of the model, excluding adjustment to the trip ends and car ownership models (WSP 2020a).

The 2018 National Road Traffic Forecasts were prepared using the NTM version known as NTMv2R for a number of scenarios, projecting traffic growth of between 17 and 51 per cent by 2050 (DfT 2018b). It was recognised that a national strategic transport model has difficulties replicating travel patterns at local levels where travel behaviour is substantially different from the national picture, particularly apparent in London where the model forecast traffic growth similar to other regions, quite contrary to historic trends.

To tackle the shortcomings of NTMv2R, a new version, NTMv5, was developed, implemented using standard commercial software (Atkins 2019). The intention is that the model should be transparent to external stakeholders, a very welcome development given the opacity of previous versions of the NTM. However, a peer review of the new version drew attention to a number of apparent shortcomings of the methodology and concluded that for London the model's projections were not convincing, for instance projecting future growth of car mode share, against the historic trend of decline (WSP 2020b). The reviewers concluded that the model could not be safely used to examine policies that relate specifically to London, and queried whether this applied more generally to rapidly growing dense urban areas across England. They took the view that the model should be suitable for use in forecasting the growth of road traffic in most areas other than those adjacent to or within major urban areas, which is a pretty major qualification, given that over 80 per cent of the British population live in urban areas.

Unexpectedly, the most recent national road traffic projections, published in 2022, were derived from the NTMv2R, not from the newer NTMv5 (DfT 2022b). This suggests a lack of confidence in the new model. These latest traffic projections show traffic growth of around 20 per cent between 2025 and 2050 for all regions, including London, which suggests that the problem of modelling road traffic in urban areas has not been resolved.

The validity of the NTM is therefore questionable. The modelling suite used to prepare the most recent projections remains complex and opaque, hence it is not possible for those other than DfT modellers and their consultants to understand what has been achieved and what has not. The peer reviews provided an exceptional opportunity to look under the bonnet, and what was found makes it questionable whether the NTM in its various versions is reliably roadworthy. And that is before the problems associated with specifying scenarios to reflect policy uncertainties, relevant to the later discussion of transport decarbonisation (in Chapter 6).

One particularly opaque component of the NTM is the National Trip End Model, the core estimate of the DfT's view of the long-term travel response to demographic and economic trends, also used extensively in transport models of all kinds. A survey of professional users found that the NTEM is seen as a 'black box', the guidance for use being complex, lengthy, technical and inaccessible; moreover, it is considered extremely challenging to understand exactly what NTEM is for, how to apply it and where an output has come from (Hive IT 2020). This lack of transparency is particularly relevant for the implications of population growth: to the extent that such growth is accommodated in new housing on greenfield sites, car use would be expected to increase, while increased housing on urban brownfield and infill sites could be better serviced by public transport; yet there is no national guidance on the spatial distribution of population growth, so that the unstated assumptions of the NTEM are particularly important for projections of travel demand.

5.4.3 Modelling rail travel

There has been a large increase in railway travel in Britain in recent years, with passenger numbers doubling between 1998 and 2018. Although the rail industry has a comprehensive database for every ticket sold, data on the characterisation of rail users is limited. Hence projections of future rail use are based on a model that relates changes in the volume of passengers travelling between a sample of stations to changes in the major drivers of rail demand, such as rail fares, GDP and quality of service; changes in household or demographic factors are not taken into account. The model, known as the Passenger Demand Forecasting Handbook, which is proprietary to the rail industry and so not open to scrutiny, substantially underpredicted actual growth in demand, indicating the existence of significant unexplained determinants (Worsley 2012).

Williams and Jahanshahi (2018) investigated these factors external to the rail industry, identifying as important structural changes in employment, particularly the shift from manufacturing to business services, and location changes of employment and of residence to city centres that benefit from rail commuting. They concluded that land use policy measures that foster urban densification, together with the land use patterns that they generate, have a major impact on the scale of transport demand and on ability of individual modes to capture and cater for this demand.

The HS2 project (discussed in section 4.16.1) developed a model (known as PLANET) to forecast passenger demand and benefits for this particular route and for parts of the conventional rail network that would be affected by the new route, which has been used to provide the economic case for the investment (HS2 2023). The model is conventional, representing multimodal supply and demand with a focus on longer distance travel. But there has been no success in developing a full model of rail use across the whole network, taking account of both internal and external determinants of demand, that would allow projections to be made of future demand.

There is some similarity here to the NTM, where exogenous determinants contribute to discrepancies between forecast and outturn. One approach to recognising future uncertainties in economic, demographic, behavioural, technological and other exogenous factors is to develop scenarios that reflect a range of such possibilities. Thus, the DfT has promulgated a set of Common Analytical Scenarios, a core scenario plus a set of seven standardised cross-modal scenarios, for use in transport forecasting and appraisal (DfT 2022b). Employing such scenarios would add substantially to the task of modelling the impact of major investments and would generate a range of outcomes in respect of benefit–cost ratios that would make it more difficult for decision makers to commit the expenditure required. Nevertheless, the principle of explicitly recognising the uncertainties inevitably involved in investment must be correct.

5.5 Time constraints

As noted earlier, it is necessary to make a variety of simplifying assumptions when constructing transport models (see section 5.2). Variable demand models may assume that the trip rate for any given demographic segment is constant through time, consistent with the findings of the National Travel Survey (TAG Unit M1, 4.3.12, 2014). The NTS also finds that average travel time remains invariant over time for settled populations generally (see section 2.3), reflecting observed time constraints on travel behaviour (Metz 2021a). So it might seem a useful simplification for the purposes of modelling to hold average travel time constant. This was the approach adopted by Zahavi (1974) in a broad-brush transport model that was applied across countries. However, this model was criticised for not performing well (Ortuzar and Willumsen 2011, 431).

Besides, a model that assumed invariant travel time would run counter to the underlying assumption of all transport models – that travel time, as a major cost, is to be minimised. For instance, the National Transport Model is based on the concept that travellers make their travel decisions by trying to minimise the cost or inconvenience (disutility) of their journeys. To achieve this, the NTM is based on a quantity termed 'Generalised Time' in which all the monetary costs (petrol, fares etc.) are converted to units of time (minutes) by dividing by the traveller's value of time, based on survey data. The converted monetary costs are added to a traveller's journey time (walking, queuing and bus, train or car ride time, etc.). Once all potential options for journeys have been converted to the single 'Generalised Time' metric, the model is then able to select the destination and mode of travel for the required journey based on the traveller's preferences, minimising overall time costs (DfT 2020b 3.9). More generally, a basic principle of traffic theory, known as Wardrop's first equilibrium, states that under equilibrium conditions, traffic arranges itself in congested networks in such a way that no vehicle can reduce its costs (time and other costs) by switching routes (Wardrop 1952). This principle is applied at the assignment stage of four-stage models (TAG M1.1 4.5.3 2024).

So a model that assumed long-run invariance of average travel time would not sit comfortably with the prevailing approach to transport modelling. Nevertheless, in the half-century since Zehavi published his model, average travel time has remained constant, consistent with the proposition that the benefits of investment that makes possible faster travel take the form predominantly of greater access to people, destinations, activities and services with the ensuing greater opportunities and choices (see section 4.12). This implies that transport models used to project long-term time savings, comparing the with- and without-investment cases, do not relate to the reality of how such interventions change travel behaviour. In effect, they project counterfactual outcomes in which travel time is constrained to be saved, in part because land use is not permitted to change, but also because of the need for modellers to provide their clients with projections that satisfy a 'realism test', which generally requires the generation of explicit time-saving benefits. The general lack of predictive validation of models by comparing forecast with outturn allows this situation to persist. More realistic models would take account of changes in land use, considered next.

5.6 Land use and transport interaction models

Changes to the transport system that lead to changes of location of where people live, work or access services – and hence in how land is used – have an impact on traffic congestion and public transport crowding, as well as on house prices and rents, and on externalities including tailpipe emissions of carbon and pollutants. To analyse the consequences, land use and transport interaction (LUTI) models have been developed, which go beyond the standard four-stage concept in that account is taken of where businesses decide to locate, where employees choose to work, where new housing may be located, and the consequences for land and property values; such models run for long periods of time to explore the interactions between the different actors (for an overview of the range of approaches see Acheampong and Silva 2015).

LUTI models cover a much broader range of behaviours than do four-stage models, which means they are harder to build and require much more data to calibrate. They are difficult to validate, given uncertainty about the extent to which observed changes in land use result from transport investment or from unrelated decisions by the actors. LUTI models are not required to be used in UK transport investment appraisal in part for these reasons, which discourages the further development of such models. Moreover, LUTI models are stated to be inconsistent with underlying theory of conventional cost-benefit analysis, so if they are used to appraise major transport schemes, the land use responses 'must be switched off' (TAG M1.1 4.7.9 2024) – surely a remarkable stipulation. The omission of land use changes means that standard transport models do not reflect real-world travel behaviour.

A more general modelling approach to recognising the full economic impact of transport changes utilises computable general equilibrium (CGE) models, also known as spatial computable general equilibrium (SCGE) models, where the spatial distribution of benefits and costs is treated. These aim to account for the distribution of impacts among every market and agent in the economy by simulating the behaviour of households, firms and others from microeconomic first principles, and have been reviewed by Robson, Wijayaratna and Dixit (2018). These authors noted that CGE models accommodate the invariance of travel time since travel demand, as well as demand in all other markets, is elastic, hence household utility in such a model will increase from a transport improvement due to increases in consumption and leisure, even if travel demand also rises as a result, thus negating the travel time savings that may be initially present.

CGE models lack transparency, even more so than four-stage models, are rarely validated, and are not generally employed in practice. An exception is an analysis of the economic case for HS2 (the standard approach was discussed at section 4.16.1). This generated very substantial real GDP impacts estimated as of the order of £2.5 billion a year in 2051 (PwC 2022). This model has also been applied to analysis the options for a third runway at Heathrow (see section 4.16.3), where the report of the study admitted that the predicted boost to GDP may be seen as large relative to the cost of investment (PwC 2014); however, the DfT took the view that the output of the model should not be used to inform decisions on account of methodological concerns (DfT 2015, 61).

Vickerman (2017) observed that CGE models are highly dependent on input assumptions, in particular how economic activity would redistribute following a major transport investment. More generally, applications of such models are one-off exercises, justified by the large scale of the proposed investments, and employ a consultant's proprietary model that typically generates benefits substantially greater than by conventional approaches, given which, they could not be said to have been influential in decision making.

5.7 Conclusions

Transport models are complex and are therefore opaque to those outside the profession of transport modellers. From the outside there are two main problems: first, the dearth of effort to demonstrate the predictive validity of models by comparing forecasts with observed outturn at a sufficient level of granularity to be able to feed back discrepancies into the calibration of the model for future use, or to question the simplifications inherent in the structure of the model, or to offer non-professionals assurance of fitness for purpose. When such comparison is possible, major discrepancies may be observed, as discussed above. Conversely, it is hard to point to instances where transport models have been demonstrated to have predictive validity, beyond perhaps the modelling of road traffic in a neighbourhood.

Second, the observed invariant average travel time implies that the long-term benefit of transport investment takes the form of access, not of travel time savings. In the short term, there may be time savings, as discussed in the motorway case studies. But in the longer term, relevant to the usual 60-year appraisal period or decarbonisation measures to achieve Net Zero, the evidence indicates that people travel further in the same amount of time as before to gain access to desired locations, activities, services and people, with the ensuing enhanced opportunities and choices. Travelling further adds to externalities, tailpipe emissions and others.

Yet time savings are the required output of four-stage and similar models used to support investment decisions, as input to the economic models that generate benefit–cost ratios. Models that project increased access would not be judged acceptable against a 'realism test'. It follows that orthodox modelling involves two counterfactuals: first, that projected in the without-investment case, which is not observable if the investment goes ahead, and is not observed in practice if it does not; and second, that projected in the with-investment case, where travel behaviour is assumed to be constrained not to take advantage of the full access benefits.

In principle, LUTI and CGE models could yield better representations of actual changes in travel behaviour and the resulting economic activity, but the problems of opacity and validation remain.

Some of the observations made in the previous chapter about the limitations of transport economics are applicable to transport modelling. The attempt to capture travel behaviour in all its diversity with limited data requires simplifications to be made and judgement exercised on the part of modelling practitioners and academics committed to the overall approach and to advancing the state of the art. Belief in the appropriateness of rigorous mathematical representation of human behaviour in transport economic analysis carries over into transport modelling, which in itself requires making simplifying assumptions for the computation to be tractable. There has been a general reluctance among practitioners to question critically what has been achieved. However, on occasion experts have revealed their anxieties.

Batty (2015), in a critique of the state of transport modelling, noted that as models have been made richer by disaggregation and by adding processes of trip decision making, they become harder to validate; he feared that the systems that models attempt to simulate are getting more complex, which means that it may not be possible to improve model performance.

Hartgen (2013), in a comprehensive critique, summarised fundamental weaknesses of travel demand modelling, based on US experience: the four-stage modelling paradigm, developed 50–60 years ago, is only a computational convenience that is not behaviourally based and does not reflect how traveller decisions are actually made; the few rigorous tests of model accuracy have not been comforting; subsequent methodological advances have increased model complexity and cost without producing significant advances in performance or understanding; invariable reliance on cross-sectional data to calibrate models contains a frozen view of travel behaviour at the time of data collection, implying unchanged future behaviour, even though the need to model reflects past changes in behaviour that require a response; limited before-and-after testing; as well as a number of detailed methodological issues. Hartgen argued for many improvements to practice, including agreed professional standards for the use of models and the treatment of uncertainty; and gathering data that goes beyond cross-sectional, using longitudinal data that tracks travel behaviour changes over time. He concluded that the four-stage process 'has not changed substantially in 60 years, and its accuracy is highly suspect', and that 'travel, activities, demographics, land use and transportation investment are so complex that it may be simply not possible to usefully forecast future travel demand'.

To supplement his book mentioned earlier (Hollander 2016), this author incisively summarised the misuse of transport models, based on his own experience and frank admissions of failure.[1] He argued that public bodies gain financial and political benefit from presenting optimistic forecasts, yet current practice does not encourage discussion of whether the forecasts give strong and relevant evidence. For their part in this state of affairs involving questionable ethics, specific charges are laid against the Department for Transport, the Treasury, Transport for London and other transport authorities, consultants, academics, professional bodies and even planning inspectors. Hollander's review failed to identify any formal body that has both the ambition and the capability to be honest about the weaknesses of the models we use. Hollander's critique has been echoed by Baldwin and Shuttleworth (2021, 38).

To add to these misgivings of the experts, there are new demands on transport modelling that would need to be accommodated: the uncertainty about long-term behaviour changes prompted by the coronavirus pandemic, in particular more working from home; the need to decarbonise the transport system, the speed of which will be driven by policy decisions; and the impact and timing of new technologies, digital navigation and ride hailing already in use, and probably automated vehicles in the future. The likely substantial but hitherto unrecognised impact of digital navigation on the modelling traffic flows has been noted earlier (section 5.4.1). Arguably, there is a generally unrecognised crisis in transport modelling. The implications will be discussed in the final chapter.

In respect of modelling generally, Helm (2023) has commented: 'Energy demand has always been difficult to forecast, not least because of changes in GDP and the composition of the economy. The performance of models has always been poor, and there is some evidence that it is getting worse.' And Sir John Kay, a distinguished business economist and commentator, has perceived a truth:

> For over ten years, I built and ran an economics consultancy business, and much of our revenue was derived from selling models to large corporate clients. One day, I asked myself a question: if these models were helpful, why did we not build similar models for our own decision making? The answer, I realised, was that our customers didn't really use these models for their decision making either. They used them internally or externally to justify decisions that they had already made (Kay 2010).

Note

1   Hollander, Y. 2015. 'Who will save us from the misuse of transport models?'. London: CTthink. [This article is no longer available.]

6
Demands of decarbonisation

6.1 Introduction

The need to tackle the challenge of climate change is well understood. The UK government has adopted, and is committed to deliver, legal obligations to achieve Net Zero carbon emissions by 2050. This involves adopting and delivering a series of five-year carbon budgets of ever reducing magnitude, with the sixth such budget, for the years 2033–7, at present the furthest into the future to be specified. This approach requires the rapid decarbonisation of the UK economy, specifically a 68 per cent reduction in greenhouse gas (GHG) emissions by 2030 and a 78 per cent reduction by 2035 (including international aviation and shipping emissions) from 1990 levels. This front-end loading is intended to achieve the main part of decarbonisation in the first half of the period to 2050, consistent with the aim of not exceeding 1.5°C degrees of warming. Plans were updated in detail in early 2023 (HM Government 2023).

Transport is the UK's largest GHG-emitting sector, responsible for a quarter of all emissions. Road transport is responsible for around 90 per cent of transport emissions, with nearly three-quarters coming from cars and vans. In the 10 years to 2019, total UK domestic emissions fell by some 25 per cent, while transport emissions fell by less than 5 per cent. Accordingly, delivering Net Zero requires a speedy shift to zero-emission vehicles, as recognised in the government's Transport Decarbonisation Plan published in 2021 (DfT 2021e). This plan also recognised the desirability of more active travel – walking and cycling – as well as more use of public transport.

There are two broad approaches to transport decarbonisation: technological change, which mainly involves replacing the internal combustion engine with electric propulsion, and behavioural change, for instance encouraging people to get out of their cars to walk or cycle.

The Department for Transport's (DfT) decarbonisation plan relies very largely on technology, avoiding the need to suggest big changes to travel behaviour, but others argue that technological change will not be sufficient and a substantial reduction in car use is unavoidable. Positions taken in this debate reflect optimism/pessimism about the pace of technological change and the scope for changes in travel behaviour. Optimism/pessimism also biases the modelling of carbon emissions. The validity of judgements of both real-world outcomes and modelling assumptions will emerge over time, but time is pressing to respond to global warming.

6.2 Technological change

The potential for new technologies to decarbonise the transport sector has been discussed previously (Metz 2019; Metz 2022a). The focus here is on implementation on timescales consistent with the policy requirements.

A general issue when discussing future technological change is the prospects for cost reduction as the technology is developed and as experience of manufacture is gained. In the early days of the development of renewables, it was judged that the UK would be well situated for wind power but not for solar power, given the limited amount of sunshine. The latter prediction turned out to be quite mistaken, not on account of a failure of weather forecasting but because of a mistaken assumption about the costs of photovoltaics, which were subsequently driven down by improvements to the technology and experience of increasing scale of production. So a question for new transport technologies is to what extent future cost reduction would be possible, based on technological advance and economies of scale through progression in manufacturing down the cost 'learning curve'. The cost of batteries for EVs is likely to benefit from both forms of progress in very competitive markets. In contrast, the cost of road and rail infrastructure based on civil engineering seems unlikely to benefit in this way. Digital technologies that help manage network operations have better prospects for cost reduction.

6.2.1 Electric propulsion for road vehicles

There is a transformative switch of propulsion of road vehicles underway, from the oil-based fuels that have been the dominant source of motive power for the past century, to electric propulsion very largely based on battery storage. This is being driven mainly by regulation, as governments see this as the best means of achieving the transformation. Thus, the UK government initially decided that there should be no new sales of petrol and diesel cars and vans after 2030, with hybrids allowed an extension to 2035, although subsequently, in September 2023, the prime minister announced deferral of the prohibition of the sale of petrol and diesel cars and vans to 2035, in line with other governments that are adopting similar policies, whether implemented by regulation or financial incentives.

Electric propulsion for cars has been pioneered by Tesla, under the leadership of Elon Musk, which has grown into a substantial manufacturer of popular battery electric vehicles (BEVs). There are other such start-up businesses in the US and China, and the traditional auto manufacturers are also making the switch. Users find these vehicles good to drive. An informed analyst reports that global sales of BEVs amounted to 14 per cent of passenger vehicles in 2022, projected to rise to 30 per cent in 2026, and to 42 per cent in Europe and 52 per cent in China, with internal combustion engine vehicles (ICEVs) now in long-term decline (BloombergNEF 2023).

The capital costs of BEVs are at present significantly higher than those of ICEVs, due to the cost of materials and manufacture of the batteries. There are offsetting savings arising from the fewer parts needed for electric motors. It is expected that battery costs will continue on a declining trajectory as improvements take place in manufacturing and as lower-cost materials become available through advances in electrochemistry. Informed estimates put cost equivalence between BEVs and ICEVs as later in the present decade (BloombergNEF 2023). In the meantime, the lower operating costs of BEVs provide an incentive to acquire these vehicles despite higher purchase costs.

One disincentive to purchase EVs is concern about the distance that can be driven with a single charge (giving rise to what is known as 'range anxiety'), coupled with uncertainty about where a charging point can be located, particularly on a longer journey. Ranges quoted by manufacturers have been increasing, currently to over 300 km on full charge. Continued improvements in battery and powertrain technologies should increase the range to meet consumer expectations, while improved charger density and charging speed could reduce range concerns in the longer term.

The minimum cost use of BEVs requires the ability to charge at home overnight. Otherwise, public charging points are needed, as they are for longer trips away from home. There is a chicken-and-egg problem here, in that a lack of public charging points deters people from purchasing EVs, while a shortage of paying customers deters commercial investment in charging points. To overcome this problem, substantial public investment is underway to increase the number of charging points, although the supply of electricity for EVs in the longer term will become entirely a commercial matter, as for fuel supply generally. Tesla has installed extensive, attractive fast charging points for its own brand of vehicles, to encourage purchasers; and recently it has agreed with other motor manufacturers to make these available to their brands, likely a significant future source of profit for Tesla.

A potential solution to the problem of range anxiety is the plug-in hybrid electric vehicle (PHEV), which has an internal combustion engine as well as a battery and electric motor, and can be charged from a charging point (the pioneering Toyota Prius was a hybrid but without the capacity for external charging, so only had the ability to capture the energy from braking to charge the battery, with very limited range under electric drive). In principle this would enable much daily driving to be carried out under electric power. However, recent evidence shows that privately owned PHEVs consume three times more petrol or diesel fuel in real-world driving than under laboratory test conditions employed to approve vehicle performance, while business users consume five times more, reflecting the lack of need to arrange electric charging (Plötz et al. 2022). So PHEVs are problematic as a pathway to incentivising the adoption of BEVs.

For larger vehicles, such as buses and trucks, the weight of the battery and the charging time for heavily used fleets may limit the use of battery-electric technology, although commercial products are on the roads. The alternative technology is the hydrogen-fuel cell electric vehicle (FCEV), which has a range comparable to diesel on a single tank of fuel, although arrangements must be made for a source of liquid hydrogen at depots. A recent analysis concluded that FCEV uptake is expected to be concentrated in high-payload HGVs, some coaches and off-road vehicles, along with some fleet vehicles where high utilisation and rapid refuelling is required, whereas lower costs are expected to drive other users to BEVs, such that FCEVs are expected to have only minor uptake for buses and regional HGVs, which will predominantly take a battery electric decarbonisation route (Faraday 2023).

For both BEV and FCEV technologies, tailpipe carbon emissions are eliminated, but there may still be carbon emissions from production of the fuel, whether gas-fired electricity generation or natural gas used to produce hydrogen. The objective of Net Zero requires that such carbon emissions be eliminated, whether by replacement by nuclear power, renewables or carbon capture and storage. However, FCEV is less efficient in utilising renewable electricity due to losses in production of hydrogen and then in converting this back to electricity on board the vehicle to drive the electric motor.

Vehicle construction involves materials, the production of which generates carbon dioxide – the smelting of iron into steel, for instance. Again, Net Zero requires that such traditional technologies are replaced with carbon-free substitutes. The means adopted to encourage this switch are emissions-trading schemes that usually work on the 'cap and trade' principle, where a cap is set on the total amount of greenhouse gases that can be emitted by sectors covered by the scheme and which decreases over time, consistent with the Net Zero objective. Within this cap, participants receive free allowances and/or buy emission allowances at auction or on the secondary market that they can trade with other participants as needed. The impact of such emissions-trading schemes is to increase over time the costs of materials, production of which releases carbon, thus incentivising carbon-free alternatives.

Consideration of both capital and lifetime operating costs allows the estimation of whole-life costs of the different classes of vehicles. Due to the UK's relatively clean electricity mix, a typical battery electric car is currently estimated to save about 65 per cent GHG emissions compared to an equivalent conventional petrol car over the lifetime, with this figure expected to improve in the future as battery technology improves and the electricity supply system is further decarbonised (Ricardo 2021).

Beyond the contribution of EVs to decarbonisation, there are wider issues of industrial policy including the UK's capacity for battery production, the supply chain of minerals and materials, recycling of batteries, the impending obsolescence of ICEVs and the future of car manufacturing, all of which will affect the availability and cost of EVs to purchasers.

6.2.2 Zero-Emission Vehicle Mandate

To implement the UK government's commitment to end the sale of new petrol and diesel cars and vans by 2035, there will be a legal requirement for a minimum percentage of each manufacturer's new car and van sales to be zero-emission each year from 2024, known as the ZEV Mandate. This will ensure future supply of vehicles and provide certainty to charge point operators and energy suppliers to coordinate the necessary investments in new technology and infrastructure. The proposed mechanism is a trading scheme whereby each year manufacturers will receive allowances to sell non-ZEV vehicles up to a given percentage of their fleet of new cars and vans, with the intention that ZEVs account for the remainder of sales (the ZEV target). Any excess non-ZEV sales must be covered by purchasing allowances from other manufacturers, or by using allowances from past or future trading periods (banking or borrowing) during the initial years of the policy. The proposed minimum ZEV target trajectory for new cars sold begins at 22 per cent in 2024, increasing to 80 per cent in 2030 and reaching 100 per cent in 2035 (DfT 2023a).

A cost–benefit analysis of the options for a ZEV mandate has been published (DfT 2023b). The preferred option was chosen to strike the best balance between driving ZEV uptake, chargepoint investment, achievability for business and affordability. This was compared with higher and lower ZEV uptake trajectories and a non-intervention scenario, all compared with a 'do-nothing' baseline. The analysis of costs distinguishes between direct impacts arising from replacing ICEVs by ZEVs, plus the cost of charging infrastructure, but assuming no behaviour change; and indirect impacts that may result from behaviour change. The latter includes additional congestion costs if the lower cost per mile of driving EVs results in more miles being driven, known as a 'rebound effect'. The analysis of benefits includes the value of carbon reductions plus air quality improvements.

The question of whether there would be behaviour change arising from lower operating costs is important. It is possible, as discussed below, that a road user charge would be introduced in time so that the operating costs of ZEVs and ICEVs would be similar. But in any event, it is unlikely that the rebound effect would be important since the per capita distance travelled by car depends mainly on three factors – speed, time available and household car ownership – none of which are changed by the switch to electric propulsion (as discussed in section 2.4). Whether or not to include a rebound effect makes a big difference to the net present value of the preferred option: £96 billion without rebound and £44 billion with rebound, reflecting the additional costs of congestion (DfT 2023b Tables 30 and 31).

Whether or not to include a rebound effect also affects the cost-effectiveness of EVs as a means to reduce carbon emissions compared to other interventions, assessed as the abatement cost to offset one tonne of carbon dioxide equivalent ($tCO2e$). For a central sensitivity case of the preferred option, the abatement cost of the ZEV Mandate for cars and vans is estimated as £12/$tCO2e$ excluding the rebound effect, and £100/$tCO2e$ including it (Tables 61 and 62).

The sensitivity of these abatement costs to assumptions about behaviour in response to a policy intervention illustrates the problem of formulating policy based on the outputs of transport or energy modelling, particularly when there are substantial uncertainties about how future travel behaviour would respond to policy interventions, as will be discussed further below.

6.2.3 Road pricing

'Road pricing' refers to charging for use of roads on a distance-related basis, familiar from toll roads in many countries where the revenue from tolls is used to reimburse the financial costs of construction. 'Road user charging' is an alternative nomenclature, but if abbreviated to 'charging' it may lead to confusion with the energy charging of EVs. 'Congestion charging' is another term employed where the main aim is to reduce road traffic congestion, as in London's congestion charge in a central zone. However, in the present context, where the focus is on reducing carbon emissions from road vehicles, 'road pricing' will be the term used. New technology would be needed to implement road pricing.

Road pricing has been a perennial issue for transport policy, seen by transport economists as a rational means for allocating scarce road capacity when congestion is prevalent (discussed in section 4.8). However, there has been a general reluctance to adopt this approach, beyond three major cities, London, Stockholm and Singapore. Nevertheless, the loss of revenue from road fuel duty accompanying the switch to electric propulsion provides a further reason to introduce road pricing. The official Office for Budget Responsibility noted that fuel duty revenue is closely linked to surface transport carbon emissions, so that as the ICEV stock is progressively replaced by electric vehicles, fuel duty receipts will follow surface transport emissions down to zero (OBR 2023). The UK government has stated that it 'will need to ensure that the tax system encourages the uptake of EVs, and revenue from motoring taxes will need to keep pace with this change, while remaining affordable for consumers' (House of Commons Transport Committee 2023). On the other hand, despite default UK government policy stating that the fuel duty rate will rise in line with RPI inflation each year, actual government policy was to freeze the rate between 2011 and 2022, and the rate is now in the third year of a temporary 5p reduction, a response to the general increase in energy costs arising from the war in Ukraine.

This experience suggests that it would be difficult politically to use road pricing to increase the costs of motoring or of road freight, as a means to reduce vehicle usage and to assist decarbonisation. Our society is too dependent on road transport, so that not many politicians would be brave enough to attempt to reduce carbon emissions by a direct increase of road fuel duty or by imposing an additional charge for road use. The situation of low-income motorists needing their cars for travelling to work would be a point of particular sensitivity.

However, since EVs do not pay fuel duty, there is a case that they should pay for use of the roads, both to contribute to the costs of operation and maintenance of the network, and to make a contribution to the Exchequer, as do ICEVs. Yet this could not be implemented immediately since the lower operating costs of EVs are important to compensate for the present higher capital costs. Nevertheless, it is expected that capital costs will decline as battery technology advances and that equivalence in capital costs of EVs and ICEs will be reached prior to the 2035 date for completion of the phasing out of sales of new ICE cars and vans.

This phasing out is a policy that commands wide support across the political spectrum, as well as from the car manufacturers and the public, who are purchasing EVs in growing numbers. There would be a good case for linking the introduction of road pricing for EVs to this policy approach, on the grounds of fairness – why should drivers of ICEVs pay more tax than drivers of EVs? There would be good time to develop a suitable road pricing system for EVs. The existing fuel duty could remain in place for ICEVs, which would avoid the anxiety that would be created, particularly among low-income motorists, by a major change in the tax regime, an approach also advocated by Corlett and Marshall (2023). EV owners are generally better off, given the newness of the technology and the limited second-hand market, and should be more able to cope with the cost increase.

There are a variety of technologies that might be used to implement road user charging, some of which are in use other countries. Yet rather than introduce an unfamiliar technology, there would be much to be said for building on London's experience, as the basis for a national system. The London congestion charge has been in operation for 20 years. It has been technically successful and publicly acceptable, with no concerns about privacy despite camera surveillance for enforcement purposes, and it generates useful net revenues that support public transport provision. London has employed the same enforcement and charging system to implement the Ultra Low Emission Zone, initially within the central congestion charging zone, expanded subsequently to encompass the area within the North and South Circular Roads with fairly minimal public opposition, and then to cover all London boroughs, albeit with some local political resistance emerging in the outer boroughs. This exemplifies the scope for incremental rollout of an established technology.

London's daily congestion charge is based on the presence of the vehicle within the charging zone, for however long. For London's technology to be the basis for a national road user charging scheme for EVs, it would be necessary to migrate the charging arrangements to a smartphone app, since a smartphone knows where it is in time and space, so knows if it is in a charging zone at a time when the charge is levied. Smartphones are generally linked to payment mechanisms. They would also need to be linked to the vehicle – since it is the presence of the vehicle that is chargeable, not the phone – which is feasible. Many European countries operate road pricing systems for trucks, in some cases employing smartphone-type technology.

Adoption of the smartphone as the mechanism for payment could be incentivised by capping the daily payment at no more than the standard daily charge as paid via the existing online payment mechanism. Once there was sufficient uptake of the app, there would be opportunity to vary the charges according to such factors as duration in the charging zone, time of day, level of congestion, location or distance travelled within the zone. This should be publicly acceptable with the daily charge cap in place, analogous to the capping of fares on London's buses and trains when contactless payments are made. The standard daily charge payable online would remain for those not wishing to use the app, as would the existing camera-based enforcement system.

With the app payment mechanism tested and accepted, it would be possible to extend it beyond the existing congestion charging zone. In the past, there had been a western extension of the London scheme, introduced by Ken Livingstone when he was mayor, but revoked by Boris Johnson, his successor. It would also be possible for other cities to adopt the technology, whether before or after national adoption for EVs. In the past both Manchester and Edinburgh developed plans to implement congestion charging, which, however, were rejected in referenda. Cambridge recently gave detailed consideration to a similar initiative, but local politicians decided not to go ahead. Adoption by a single city may seem a major step by the voters, whereas taking advantage of a national road pricing system in prospect may lessen their reluctance.

A national scheme of road pricing applied to EVs could be introduced incrementally, whether by road type (such as motorways) or by region, and by starting the charge at a low level, increasing over time as the arrangements bed down. While a national scheme might employ a separate payment app from that used in London or other cities, arguably it would make more sense to use a single payment mechanism, apportioning the revenues between the Exchequer and the highway authorities, allowing the latter scope to vary their component of the price charged to meet local needs. Over time, this could reduce the need for local authorities to bid competitively to central government for funding local transport initiatives, consistent with a general policy trend to increasing devolution of responsibilities from national to local government.

One particular possibility for the exercise of local decisions on the local component of revenue would be to fund improvements to public transport by increasing the level of charge, subject to the willingness of the electorate. More and better bus and rail services would be important in providing an alternative to car use, so facilitating decarbonisation. However, fare box revenues are generally insufficient to support good local public transport services, in respect of both frequency and geographical spread, so external funding is required. Yet subsidy from government, whether national or local, will always be in short supply. Revenues from road pricing would be a feasible source of further support to improve local bus and rail services.

The phasing out of sales of new ICEVs over the next 10 years is generally agreed to be feasible in terms of EV supply, but faster decarbonisation could be achieved by employing the revenues from EV road pricing to fund a scrappage scheme for ICEVs. This would need to be targeted at the most carbon-emitting vehicles, a function of engine size and distance travelled. Age would also be important since the amount payable per vehicle would become more attractive as vehicles became older and less valuable. However, such a scrappage scheme could not usefully be implemented until there were good numbers of EVs available in the used car market as replacements for scrapped ICEVs.

6.2.4 Road investment and innovation

Governments generally see investment in new road capacity as desirable, as a means to tackle road traffic congestion and improve connectivity across the economy, which, it is believed, would boost productivity (see section 4.16). Yet adding capacity must increase vehicle-miles travelled, and, while ICEVs predominate, must increase associated externalities, in particular carbon emissions. Hence there is a conflict between two policies, both of which command wide support.

The DfT, responsible for the strategic road network in England, has promulgated a succession of investment plans, known as Road Investment Strategies, that commit funds for five-year periods, to allow its operating arm, National Highways, to plan ahead. When individual schemes are considered at planning inquiries, it has been the practice for the additional carbon emissions to be described as 'de minimis', so providing only a small offset to the estimated benefits arising from the supposed saving of travel time. The Department's Transport Decarbonisation Plan, published in 2021 (DfT 2021e), promised a review of the National Networks National Policy Statement, which sets out policy for investment in road and rail networks so that national issues need not be considered at local planning inquiries for particular schemes. However, a draft of a new such statement issued in 2023 retained the focus on individual schemes (DfT 2023c), imposing no requirement to estimate the carbon emissions from the five-year programmes, which would likely be significant in offsetting the carbon reduction benefits of EV introduction.

The Welsh government commissioned an independent panel to review its road construction programme, and largely accepted its advice, such that future investment would be in schemes that support modal shift and reduce carbon emissions, as well as improving safety and adapting to the impact of climate change (Welsh Government 2023). However, such a reconciliation between road investment and Net Zero has not yet been achieved in England.

Accordingly, a question is whether there are alternatives to the civil engineering technologies that add capacity and thus increase carbon emissions. Are there technologies that enable improved efficiency of the road network without increasing carbon emissions? Digital navigation, commonly known as satnav in the roads context, was discussed earlier as one of the four important new transport technologies deployed or in development (section 2.4). It was also referred to in section 5.4.1 as a likely contributor to the underestimation of road traffic growth following motorway widening, the consequence of local users diverting to a widened motorway to take advantage of faster journey times.

More generally, the widespread adoption of digital navigation by road users is affecting travel behaviour, albeit in ways that are not fully appreciated as yet (Metz 2022b). As well as diverting local users to new major road capacity intended for longer-distance business users, thereby detracting from the forecast economic benefits of the investment, there is general experience of diversion of traffic from congested major roads to minor roads that provide less congested alternatives – minor roads that previously were used only by those with local knowledge. Such increases in traffic on minor roads have detrimental environmental consequences for those living in neighbourhoods so affected, as well as deterring active travel for which minor roads are well suited, and being in direct conflict with the intention of policies such as Low Traffic Neighbourhoods that aim to reduce local car use and encourage walking and cycling.

On the other hand, a positive benefit of digital navigation is the forecasting of estimated journey time in the light of prevailing and expected traffic conditions. This enables those road users who need to be at their destination at a specified time to decide when best to set out, while those who are more flexible can avoid the most congested traffic conditions. Road traffic congestion has proved difficult to tackle by road enlargement, for reasons discussed previously (see section 4.8), hence the truth of the maxim that we can't build our way out of congestion. Mitigating the main perceived detrimental impact of congestion – the unpredictability of journey time – by the use of digital navigation is the best means available for tackling congestion. The further potential of digital navigation to provide a better experience for road users will be discussed in the next chapter.

6.2.5 Rail investment

The UK rail network is only partly electrified: although only 38 per cent of routes are electrified, 71 per cent of passenger rolling stock is electric (ORR 2022). For new capacity on main routes, such as HS2, electric propulsion would be the norm. For lesser-used passenger and freight routes, the cost of conventional electrification may be unjustifiable. Alternatives under development to the present diesel-fuelled propulsion are hydrogen-fuel cell and battery electric propulsion.

In principle, mode switch from road to rail could be helpful for decarbonisation. However, although HS2 has low carbon emissions per passenger kilometre, in part the result of such mode shift, when the embedded carbon in constructing the new route is taken into account, there is estimated to be a positive net carbon footprint (HS2 2013, section 5.6). Electrification of existing routes would provide a net carbon benefit in respect of operational emissions, although when the construction costs of traction power are taken into account, the range of net present value outcomes has been projected to be predominantly negative (Network Rail 2020, section 6). Nevertheless, electrification of existing routes based on established technology is cost-effective compared with decarbonising air travel. There is also scope for making better operation use of existing rail infrastructure through digital signalling and control systems that allow shorter safe headways between trains, hence increasing effective capacity (Network Rail 2018).

6.2.6 Air travel

Aviation is the most difficult transport sector to decarbonise. There are two broad technological approaches. First, to replace kerosene derived from oil with alternatives, known as sustainable aviation fuels

(SAF), which comprise biofuels, including recycled cooking oil and derived from agricultural wastes, or synthetic kerosene derived from hydrogen generated from renewable electricity and CO_2 captured from the atmosphere or from industrial sources. These possibilities yield fuel suitable for existing aircraft. Second, to design and build new aircraft types that use either batteries with electric motors or hydrogen as energy sources; however, due to the weight of batteries, electric aircraft seem likely to be limited to short-range services, while the feasibility of liquid hydrogen-powered aircraft over longer ranges has yet to be demonstrated (Transport & Environment 2022).

The high costs and limited availability of SAFs are constraints on their use. The UK government is to mandate that at least 10 per cent of aviation fuel is to be made from sustainable resources by 2030. This is intended to generate demand, provide incentives to producers to invest, and help close the gap between the price of SAF and that of fossil kerosene (DfT 2023d). It seems likely that the largest share of carbon abatement from aviation will result from the introduction of SAFs, but huge efforts by governments and the international industry would be needed to reduce annual emissions from the sector to zero by 2050 without managing demand for air travel (Graver et al. 2022). Offsetting carbon emissions through investment in sectors that store energy, such as forestry, seems infeasible on the scale required and does not deal with the contribution to global warming from contrail-induced cloud formation (Kallbekken and Victor 2022). Altogether, the scope for new technology to reduce aviation's contribution to climate change seems particularly problematical, yet because the need is very pressing, useful progress may turn out to be possible.

6.3 Behaviour change

Many analysts and policymakers take the view that reliance on technological change would be insufficient to meet the agreed trajectory to achieve Net Zero by 2050, with the bulk of decarbonisation required in the first half of the period. For instance, the Scottish Government aspires to reduce car kilometres by 20 per cent by 2030 (Scottish government 2020, 3.3.19). In contrast, the DfT does not assume that any reduction in car-kilometres travelled is necessary to fulfil its climate change objectives (DfT 2022b).

While reducing car use would undoubtedly be helpful, the question of its feasibility is debatable. The phenomenon of car dependence was discussed in Chapter 1, both the utility of the car as a convenient mode for door-to-door travel and the attractions of car ownership for reasons beyond utility (see section 1.3). For travel between locations where there is no convenient alternative mode, utility is sufficient to account for choice of the car. Where other modes are available, utility may still be the main motivation, on account of door-to-door speed and other convenience factors, although positive feelings may reinforce use of a car. Even when the car is the slower option, those with positive feelings about car ownership may prefer to drive.

From this perspective, there are a number of possible approaches to reducing car dependence that broadly fall into three categories: providing acceptable alternative modes of travel, and making car use less attractive than the alternatives – the carrot and the stick. And then there is the possibility of lessening the good feelings about car ownership and use (Metz 2023a).

6.3.1 Alternatives to car travel

Criticism is often voiced when new housing on greenfield sites is planned without alternatives to use of the car. A question that arises is whether those who purchase these homes feel deprived on that account, or whether they choose to live in such locations because they are positive about driving and are pleased to have plenty of parking space for their cars. While there have been investigations into how attitudes, behaviours and residential choices influence choice of sustainable travel options in urban areas, empirical investigation has been lacking to understand to what extent a new greenfield housing development results in involuntary car dependence – with deprivation for those residents who do not have access to a car – and, conversely, to what extent requiring developers to make provision for active travel and public transport would reduce car use. Given that these developments are built to sell, it is possible that most purchasers are content with a car-based lifestyle.

The situation of travel to and from new greenfield housing is a subset of travel in rural areas, where limited public transport provision is in competition with the car that allows door-to-door journeys, which serves to limit demand and hence frequency of bus services, and which therefore may require public subsidy. Indeed, it may be said that car dependence helps avoid rural depopulation, in that without the car enabling journeys from home to work and other essential trips, people would leave villages for towns and cities – not generally a problem in Britain but experienced in countries with lower population densities such as Spain and France.

The converse of greenfield housing without alternatives to the car is new city apartments with no provision for parking – not uncommon in some inner London boroughs at least. In the US this is known as transit-oriented development, where housing is constructed on sites within walking distance of new rail-based transit schemes. There is an extensive literature on the topic of transport-related residential self-selection – whether people choose to live in neighbourhoods that align with their prior travel preferences, or whether their behaviour changes as a result of the better access to transit. A recent review highlights the complexity, heterogeneity and uncertainty of research findings (Guan, Wang and Cao 2020).

While the planning of new settlements should include consideration of provision of alternative modes of travel to the car, the greater problem concerns the existing built environment that has developed over the period since the middle of the last century as car ownership has become widespread. The result has been relatively low-density development in Britain, where the car has facilitated access to people and places, allowing dispersion of opportunities for access to employment, housing, services and activities, as well as to family and friends. This is not the ultra-low density of sprawling US cities, but equally not the high residential density of admired European cities such as Paris or Barcelona. The British generally appreciate family houses with gardens, such that the resulting low density limits public transport provision (Rodrigues and Breach 2021).

In these circumstances, the scope for the planning system to reduce car dependence is very limited, particularly since the vast share of property, both residential and commercial, is owned privately. Besides, homeowners value attractive neighbourhoods and could not afford the cost of rebuilding. Hence the ability to reduce car use through the creation of '15-minute cities' or '20-minute neighbourhoods' is for the most part more of an aspiration than a reality in existing built environments.

Nevertheless, there are many suggested innovations and initiatives aimed at getting people out of their cars by providing what is hoped are attractive alternatives. A comprehensive process to develop what is known as a Sustainable Urban Mobility Plan has been supported by the European Union, in which context reduction of greenhouse gas emissions is one of many objectives (Rupprecht Consult 2019).

Promotion of active travel – walking and cycling – and of public transport as alternatives to car use is widely seen as central to decarbonisation of road transport. Yet, as noted in Chapter 1, cities such as Copenhagen, with strong cycling cultures, have relatively low levels of public transport use (see section 1.3.1). Car use in Copenhagen is only slightly less than in London. So it is difficult to get people out of their cars onto bicycles, for the reasons discussed earlier. Consistent with this perspective, the DfT's guidance for the appraisal of cycle investments, based on a review of evidence, stipulates a car–cycle diversion factor of 0.24, meaning that if there were to be 100 new cyclists, there would be 24 fewer people travelling by car (TAG A5.1 2022, 3.7.3). The corollary is that 76 per cent would switch from other modes, i.e. from public transport and walking.

Also consistent with the conclusion that getting people to switch from the car to active travel is difficult are the estimates in the DfT's Transport Decarbonisation Plan, where carbon reduction estimated from increased walking and cycling is put at 1–6 $MtCO2e$ for the period 2020–50, which is very small and implies much uncertainty, in comparison with that projected from policies to decarbonise cars and vans, 620–850 $MtCO2e$ over the same period.

Whereas walking is commonly lumped together with cycling in the decarbonisation context, walking is the slowest mode of travel, and while good for health, it is most limiting in the access made possible by this mode of travel. Hence no substantial increase in walking seems likely.

A general problem in aiming to reduce carbon emissions by encouraging mode switch to cycling is that 80 per cent of carbon emissions from UK car journeys arise from trips of more than five miles, and likewise to switch to walking given that 95 per cent of car emissions arise from trips of more than two miles (DfT 2009, fig 2.7).

There are, nevertheless, particular opportunities to shift usage away from the car. For instance, 37 per cent of children in Britain are taken to school by car and only 2 per cent cycle (NTS 2019, Table 0613). In Copenhagen, 25 per cent of children travel to school by bicycle, although a not insignificant 18 per cent are taken by car (City of Copenhagen 2019). To decrease the school run in Britain, parents would wish to be assured of safe cycling routes and may need to accept some reduction in choice of schools.

There are a number of technological innovations that, it is hoped, would encourage mode shift away from car use, including electric bikes, electric scooters and shared car use made possible by digital platforms (both short-term rental and shared journeys), and demand-responsive travel (DRT, mostly in the form of minibuses summoned via a smartphone app). Based on available evidence, including of both new and withdrawn services, these innovations seem likely to fill niches in the travel market, rather than be transformative. This is in part because they are in competition with the individually owned car and its attractions of both utility and ownership, as well as with existing public transport with published timetables, important for journeys to work and school.

For these reasons the commercial prospects seem generally insufficiently attractive to private investors, while the possibility of continuing public subsidy seems limited, given pressures on public-sector budgets generally. Thus, Currie and Fournier (2020), reviewing the evidence, find a high failure rate of DRTs, suggesting they are still a high-cost, experimental, uncertain and unreliable solution for cities. Accordingly, the magnitude of carbon reduction from these innovative technologies appears very likely to be quite small.

One innovation that has appeared especially attractive is mobility-as-a-service (MaaS), which aspires to offer a full range of alternatives to the private car. In practice, this has been difficult to implement, in part on account of the operational complexity of a multimodal offering, and in part because of the reluctance of existing transport operators to participate. Vij and Dühr (2022), reviewing experience, concluded that the benefits from MaaS are still somewhat speculative, highly localised and frequently contextual, while presenting a threat to existing service providers, as integration with other services that are potentially in competition with their own core offering could adversely impact profitability and cost recovery. These authors find that in many cases similar benefits can be realised through information and communication technologies that do not require integration with other services.

The best technological alternative to car travel is rail-based public transport, in all its forms, from street-running light rail (trams) to heavy rail on existing or new track, whether over- or underground – a back-to-the-future approach. Rail is an attractive alternative to cars, buses and taxis on congested roads in respect of speed and reliability, which is an important reason for its resurgence in recent years. However, rail is expensive and new routes are dislocating to existing communities, yet once built are rarely regretted. Britain is relatively poorly provided with urban metro systems, which means there are opportunities for decarbonisation by mode switch away from cars. But public subsidy of capital costs and, for urban rail, of operating costs would be needed.

There has been recent interest in increasing the use of public transport by offering free travel or markedly lower fares, although the evidence is that modal shift from cars is difficult to achieve by this means, with most of any increase in usage coming from those who previously walked or cycled (UITP 2020). A popular scheme in Germany offered unlimited travel on regional rail, trams and buses for nine euros a month during the summer of 2022 and was used by nearly half the population, substantially boosting rail use, particularly in rural areas at weekends, but not getting people out of cars (Quinio 2022).

6.3.2 Reducing the attractions of car use and ownership

To complement the availability of hopefully appealing alternatives to the car, there is scope for making car use less attractive. Interventions may reduce distances travelled by car, but the larger effect is likely to be to change the mode of travel.

Urban car use is made less attractive by constraints on parking, including limiting parking at the kerbside to permit unloading of goods vehicles and setting down from taxis; likewise, reducing carriageway available for general traffic by conversion to bus and cycle lanes and pedestrian space. Low-traffic neighbourhoods constitute area-wide efforts to reduce car use. Raising charges for parking also discourages car use, both on-street and off-street facilities controlled by local authorities. A workplace parking levy, as implemented in Nottingham, UK, can discourage commuting by car while generating revenue to fund public transport (Dale et al. 2019).

Road pricing deters car use, as implemented in London, Stockholm and Singapore (Metz 2018). In London and Stockholm, this has been confined to central areas, with limited impact on traffic in the wider metropolitan areas. Singapore, as a city state without a rural hinterland, has always levied a high charge for entitlement to car ownership, to limit the number of vehicles to the capacity of the road network, so that car ownership is about 100 per thousand population, compared with more than four times that number in other developed countries. Some Chinese cities have also limited car ownership, whether by auction of entitlements, as in Singapore, or by lottery. The implication is that using road pricing to achieve a substantial reduction on car use would require much higher prices than charged in London or Stockholm, likely only achievable by a political regime that felt secure in power.

Road fuel taxation adds to the cost of motoring, with quite wide variations between countries. However, high taxation tends to encourage use of smaller vehicles, which, while good for carbon reduction, is modest compared with the switch of technology to electric propulsion.

As well as making car use less attractive through such measures as discussed above, there is the possibility of reducing car ownership if a better understanding were available of why ownership is attractive, quite apart from utility in travel, as discussed in section 1.3.2. Feelings of pride in car ownership vary widely across countries for reasons that are not apparent, beyond the status associated with ownership in developing economies. Attitudes also vary within countries, with younger adults in developed economies making less use of cars, particularly when living, working and studying in or near attractive city centres. More generally, concerns about the environmental detriments arising from car use prompt some to give up their cars, although it is difficult to predict how far such a movement might spread, particularly as the switch to electric vehicles reduces environmental anxieties. Nevertheless, the marketing efforts of the highly competitive car industry will continue to identify motivations for the purchase and use of cars, while the engineering side will continue to innovate to develop more attractive products. The aim of these efforts is to instil positive feelings about car purchase and use, which tend to trump the countervailing efforts to reduce car dependence. The innovations associated with the current switch to electric propulsion yield vehicles attractive to drive, as well as receiving the endorsement of governments through financial incentives to purchase, including lower rates of taxation, and support for provision of electric charging facilities. More generally, the governments of countries in which car manufacturers and their supply chains are located are supportive of these businesses and their outputs, for reasons of both employment and industrial policy.

Attitudes to the car are part of a wider debate about the role of consumption in society, including whether current levels of consumption of goods are sustainable, the role of repair and recycling, and concepts such as the 'circular economy'. In this context, a better understanding is needed of how favourable behaviour change may be achieved, for instance within the COM-B framework, which posits that to change, an individual must have the capability, the opportunity and the motivation (Michie, Van Stralen and West 2011), and which has been widely used in the public health context (Public Health England 2020). Behaviour change techniques have been applied with success to improving road safety (RAC Foundation 2017). In contrast, a systematic review found no evidence of efficacy of behavioural interventions aimed at reducing car trips (Arnott et al. 2014). Nevertheless, the Scottish government has stated that it has considered interventions to reduce car use in the context of the COM-B model of behaviour change, although no detail is provided (Transport Scotland 2022, 21). The difficulty may be a lack of motivation to give up the car, in contrast to motivation to switch to electric propulsion.

Altogether, the realistic scope for reducing car ownership and use in developed economies with the aim of cutting carbon emissions seems quite limited. The best opportunities are in cities where rail-based public transport is most economically feasible and where population density means that catchment areas, whether for schools or supermarkets, are tighter, making active travel more attractive. But the opportunities for increasing urban population density are limited by the ownership of property being very largely private, by the attractions of existing neighbourhoods for residents, and by the unaffordability of rebuilding most existing housing. The planner's concept of 'gentle densification' sounds attractive, yet while planning policies may encourage higher urban densities and neighbourhoods that are well provided with services, thus obviating the need for longer journeys, the impact of such policies will generally be limited.

The experience of the coronavirus pandemic, discussed in Chapter 3 showed that people were willing to forgo travel on a substantial scale, motivated by personal concern for health and imposed public health measures. But once the threat receded, travel demand resumed, most rapidly by private car, more slowly by public transport. And while there seem to be some long-term impacts on the pattern of demand, notably more working from home, car use overall remains as attractive as before.

6.3.3 Reducing air travel

As discussed in Chapter 3, demand for leisure air travel surged after pandemic restrictions were lifted and the epidemic faded, albeit business travel has been slower to revive. The scope for limiting future demand growth is problematic, let alone reducing demand below current levels. Ceasing airport expansion would help (see section 4.16.3). France has banned domestic short-haul fights where rail alternatives exist; that might be considered in the UK, where domestic passengers comprised some 14 per cent of all air travellers, although this includes travel to Northern Ireland and more distant Scottish destinations.

The cost of air travel might be increased to inhibit demand growth. Aviation fuel is untaxed, the consequence of a long-standing international agreement. Air Passenger Duty is charged per passenger flying from UK airports, varying with distance and class of travel – £200 for the longest flights at a class above the lowest on the aircraft. The European Union is applying the EU Emission Trading Scheme (ETS) solely to CO_2 emissions from intra-EU flights, but aims to extend it to all flights into and out of the EU unless better international arrangements emerge. The UK's ETS applies to domestic flights and flights to EU states. An ETS requires total carbon emissions to be reduced over time; participants receive or buy allowances that must be surrendered to cover their emissions, so that the price of allowances will rise, affecting the cost of air travel over time. However, the impact on demand for air travel depends on many factors, including the precise design of the UK ETS and its relation with other such schemes, which at this stage are unclear (for detailed discussion see Frontier Economics 2022).

So, in summary, relying on behaviour change to deliver a substantial part of transport decarbonisation seems to reflect considerable optimism bias, given the impediments discussed above.

6.4 Modelling decarbonisation

Whether or not a package of policy measures would achieve the desired rate of decarbonisation of the transport sector (or any other) requires modelling outcomes projected out to 2050, taking into account future costs (which depend on technology development), uptake of new technologies by users (which depends in part on investment in complementary technologies such as charging points for EVs), performance of new technologies (for instance, range of battery EVs) and financial and tax incentives offered by governments, as well as many possibilities for behaviour change. Thus modelling future carbon emissions is a demanding and uncertain business.

There are broadly two approaches to modelling transport decarbonisation. First, modelling the whole energy sector allows carbon emissions to be projected, from which transport carbon emissions can be pulled out. This is the approach used by the UK government, with the Department for Energy Security and Net Zero in the lead, and involves good collaboration with the academic community; the Climate Change Committee, the government's official advisor, is also a major user (Li and Strachan 2021).

Second, transport modelling, as outlined in Chapter 5, can be the basis for estimation of future transport sector carbon emissions. Such estimation by the DfT may employ the National Transport Model, sector-specific models for aviation and maritime, and ad hoc models. Generally, these models are not transparent, nor is the academic community involved.

A range of findings has emerged from modelling decarbonisation of the transport sector. Some approaches identify a requirement for significant behavioural change, in particular a reduction in car travel, as well as a shift to electric propulsion. These include the Sixth Carbon Budget of the Climate Change Committee (2020) and Marsden (2023). On the other hand, neither the DfT's Transport Decarbonisation Plan (DfT 2021e) nor other UK government projections assume a reduction in car travel. The International Council on Clean Transportation (2020) projects measures necessary to decarbonise the global transport sector through technological change, without the need for measures that may slow or decrease the current trajectory for transportation demand.

Lam and Wengraf (2023) employed a purpose-built model that projects the population of cars on UK roads to answer the question whether it is necessary to reduce car mileage to meet our carbon emission goals. They concluded that while such a reduction has the greatest impact, it is not an absolute prerequisite, so that policy approaches which do not involve such a reduction would depend much more on the achieving both a high rate of uptake of BEVs and a high rate of exit of ICEVs.

Inevitably, optimism/pessimism bias informs the modelling of transport decarbonisation. As noted earlier (in section 5.3), the predictive validity of such models for projections of traffic flows and of economic benefit is unproven. The question of model validity must also apply to carbon emissions. What would be helpful is transparency and collaboration between modellers to better understand the reasons for different projections, as has happened for the epidemiological modelling of the coronavirus pandemic. The collaboration with academia for energy modelling is a good precedent, as is the availability of the Treasury's model of the UK economy for use by non-government bodies. The collaborative, international modelling of climate change, as input to the work of the Intergovernmental Panel on Climate Change, is another example of transparent modelling allowing challenge and debate. Were there to be a need to instigate potentially unpopular changes in travel behaviour based on the projections of models, it would be helpful if there were consensus among modellers, endorsed by informed experts.

Nevertheless, even with consensus, modelling long-term transport-sector carbon emissions falls short of providing a firm basis for near-term policy decisions. Rather, it indicates a direction of movement and a range of possible outcomes. Arguably the best approach we have to decision making is the present UK system of setting forward five-year carbon budgets, based on the independent advice of the Climate Change Committee, that reflect both achievement to date and interventions required to meet future policy requirements, Net Zero in particular, to which the government responds.

Thus, the government's Carbon Budget Delivery Plan of March 2023 provided a detailed account of its proposals, policies and projections, leading to the stated confident conclusion that the requirements of the sixth carbon budget (2033–7) could be met through a combination of the quantified and unquantified policies identified (HM Government 2023, 15). Yet the subsequent response of the Climate Change Committee was critical, seeing a general lack of urgency and leadership in the government's approach, and in the case of transport, the committee was concerned that policies that aim to incentivise a shift from cars to more sustainable modes have been switched from the quantified category to unquantified, implying a lack of commitment (Climate Change Committee 2023, 108). However, as discussed previously (see sections 1.3.1 and 6.3.1), it has proved difficult to achieve mode shift away from cars, and moreover, a study commissioned by the committee on this topic did not suggest that specifying quantifiable achievement would be straightforward (WSP 2023), so caution in quantification is warranted.

6.5 Conclusions

Decarbonisation is a high-level strategic objective for the transport sector. There are good prospects for substantial contributions from technological solutions for surface transport despite uncertainty about the pace of change that may be feasible. Aviation is much more difficult.

In contrast, the scope for effecting behavioural change to reduce transport carbon emissions is quite limited in a democratic society, despite the enthusiasm of proponents of active travel and other alternatives to the car. More vigorous measures than those discussed above are possible, for instance a substantial increase in the cost of oil-derived fuels. But this would come into the category of measures envisaged by Jean-Claude Juncker, former president of the European Commission, when he said: 'We all know what to do, but we don't know how to get re-elected once we have done it.'

As well as the uncertainties about technological and behavioural changes, there are uncertainties arising from the complex and opaque nature of the modelling employed to project the future impact of policy measures. These uncertainties taken together argue for a stepwise approach to decarbonisation, maintaining momentum while recognising lead times of technological developments and behavioural interventions.

The political scope for transport decarbonisation measures is affected by what is going on in other sectors, such as home heating and agriculture, where progress is slower, and also by actions in other countries, given that rising atmospheric carbon levels are a global problem, and that coal-fired power stations are still being built in some countries. On the other hand, evidence of climate change in the form of increasing frequency and intensity of storms, floods, wildfires and the like increases the case for action. So policy must evolve to respond, while technology continues to develop and possibilities for behavioural change enlarge.

7
Fresh approaches to travel analysis and policy

7.1 Introduction

The established methodologies for transport economic appraisal and modelling have been found wanting, as discussed in previous chapters. The key assumption has been that the benefits of investment in the transport system largely take the form of the saving of travel time to users, so that appraisal and modelling have developed to be consistent with that assumption. However, the evidence of how travel behaviour has changed as a result of the availability of faster means of travel is that the benefits are taken as increased access to people and places, activities and services, with the ensuing enhanced opportunities and choices.

Moreover, orthodox methodologies have become excessively elaborate on the supposition that attempting to include all relevant variables would generate more reliable outcomes. Yet as argued earlier, the validity of transport models remains unproven, and indeed they are misleading, given the effective requirement of economists for user benefits in the form of time savings. We therefore need analytical approaches that are based on evidence of actual travel behaviour and that are accordingly more relevant to decision making. These would helpfully include heuristics, rules of thumb, that would provide assistance for decision makers in the public sector who are concerned to improve the transport system's ability to meet people's needs for access.

At the same time as recognition of the importance of access benefits has emerged, the need to decarbonise the transport system has become a pressing policy concern, which makes it problematic to increase transport capacity in order to permit travel demand growth where that would increase fossil fuel use.

To chart a way forward, let us recapitulate some of the main conclusions of the earlier chapters:

- Almost two centuries of growth of per capita distance travelled ceased around the turn of the century, resulting in a high proportion of travel by car, the consequence of the access benefits this mode provides, and despite the detrimental outcomes for the environment and for social interactions.
- This cessation of growth of travel can be associated with both a lack of further technological opportunities for faster travel, and with the saturation of demand for travel. New technologies are unlikely to allow significantly faster travel.
- It would be difficult for active travel or public transport to claim a substantially larger share of travel supply in the future, beyond city centres.
- Average travel time, at about an hour a day, is a long-term invariant for settled populations. Estimation of the economic benefits of transport investment based on the saving of travel time is therefore misleading.
- While travel time has remained unchanged, the growth of average per capita distance travelled over the past two centuries implies that the benefits of investment – private investment in cars and public investment in roads and railways – have been taken as improved access to people, places, services and activities, with the ensuing greater range of opportunities and choices.
- Access benefits, which are subject to diminishing returns, have proved difficult to monetarise for the purposes of cost–benefit analysis.
- Transport models are complex and opaque, requiring expert judgement about parameter values, with the likelihood of bias such that projections conform to clients' expectations. Validation of predictive performance is rare, which limits confidence in the use of models for estimating the economic benefits of transport investments or carbon emissions associated with policy measures.
- Transport models that project travel time savings, comparing with- and without-investment cases, do not recognise that users take the benefit of investment as access benefits, travelling further in the time available, with increased externalities related to vehicle-miles travelled as well as changes in land use.
- The coronavirus pandemic had a large impact, but subsequently travel behaviour reverted very largely to what it had been previously, particularly by car.

- The need to decarbonise the transport sector has become an overarching strategic policy requirement. Hitherto, it has proved difficult to articulate strategic policies with meaningful economic content for the transport sector as a whole or for road, rail and air investment.

7.2 System maturity

To respond to the above conclusions, we need to assess what further development of the transport system could be justified, economically, socially and environmentally. Britain, like most developed economies, has extensive road and rail networks, as well as international and regional airports, all of which need to be well maintained. In developing economies, new transport infrastructure investment can unlock economic growth through improving access to, within and between urban areas. However, in developed economies the benefits of further investment are marginal, and the costs are high, implying that there could be better ways of spending public money.

There is therefore a good case for a presumption that, in general, the transport network is mature, consistent with the evidence for travel demand saturation (see section 2.5). Hence further investment in costly additional infrastructure would require a convincing case to be argued for specific projects. The presumption of maturity is already the case for urban roads, where, in the last century, investment in increased capacity in the form of both new (often elevated) roads and enlarged carriageway for vehicles took place in response to growing car ownership; whereas more recently the trend has been to recover such capacity for active travel and prioritised bus routes. Demand for vehicle travel on urban roads must now be managed within constrained capacity. It is remarkable that the Department for Transport's Transport Analysis Guidance has very limited coverage of interventions to manage urban traffic, given that over 80 per cent of the population live in urban areas: no consideration is given to the economic and other impacts of parking management, congestion charging, public transport subsidy, support for micro-mobility, clean air zones, Low Traffic Neighbourhoods or installation of public electric charging points.

In the case of airports, while there are plans to increase capacity by building additional or enlarged runways and terminals at Heathrow and elsewhere, the day-to-day business focuses on improving operational efficiency. Airlines maximise use of aircraft, passenger occupancy and use of allocated airport slots, while minimising operating costs; airports maximise passenger throughput; and the air traffic control authorities optimise the use of crowded airspace. The main professional discipline is operations research, rather than civil engineering, which is the dominant discipline of interurban road authorities. As noted earlier, there is a good case for not adding to airport capacity since the value of the marginal leisure trip is quite low (see section 4.16.3).

Economic analysis of interurban road investment contrasts with the operational economics of the management of mature networks. There is a good argument for treating the interurban road network as mature, so not aiming to invest to increase capacity generally, hitherto justified by notional travel time savings generated by models that have not been validated predictively. There may be benefits from particular investments associated with land use change; for instance, were a third runway at Heathrow airport to be built, investment in surface transport infrastructure would be needed to cope with increased passenger numbers, the cost of which should form part of the cost of the project as a whole (see section 4.16.3). More generally, location-specific road investment to make land accessible for development could be justified where the decision to develop is made jointly by planners, developers and transport authorities and where the developer contributes to the cost of the infrastructure. The case would be based more on commercial considerations than on orthodox welfare economics, although externalities should be taken into account (see also section 7.5 below).

There is also a good case for public investment in EV public charging points, to accelerate the electrification of the vehicle fleet, as well as for investment in digital technologies to increase the operational efficiency of the road network, discussed below.

The case for public investment in the railways is not in conflict with decarbonisation since, in general, electric propulsion would be employed, and some mode shift away from road use may be achieved. Yet much rail investment is driven by social and political considerations, rather than by evident economic benefits, as discussed earlier (see section 4.16.1). And while there is a case for investing in urban rail to increase agglomeration benefits, both to business and consumers, the impact of the coronavirus pandemic has raised a question about the magnitude of such benefits (see section 3.2).

Cessation of investment in a national road construction programme would be a big shift of policy politically, although this is what the Welsh government has decided (see section 4.18). There is still widespread support for road investment among most politicians, national and local, the latter because the funds provided by central government are seen as 'free money'. It is widely supposed that increasing road capacity reduces congestion, improves connectivity and boosts economic growth, although the basis for this supposition is tenuous (see section 4.8). And of course, the construction industry and the consultancies that benefit from the funds that flow are also supportive. Nevertheless, there is a strong case for a switch in focus from civil engineering to digital technologies, as discussed next.

7.3 Management of mature road networks

For railways and air travel, access to the infrastructure is managed. Headways between trains are managed for safety reasons, even though on most routes there is no constraint on passenger numbers and crowding. For aviation, both headways between aircraft at busy airports and passenger numbers on aircraft are managed. But the highways are generally open to all (subject to prohibitions on cyclists and pedestrians on fast motor roads), and so congestion is a consequence, which needs to be managed.

Road traffic congestion arises in or near areas of population density, whether urban or peri-urban, where car ownership is high, such that there is insufficient road capacity for all the vehicle trips that might be made. Some potential users are deterred by the prospect of unacceptable delays and make alternative decisions: a different route or time of travel, a different destination or mode of travel where feasible, or not to travel at all. If the capacity of the congested road is increased, delays are reduced, and these previously deterred road users are attracted back onto the network, restoring congestion to what it had been before the increase in capacity. This additional traffic is known generally as 'induced traffic', some cases of which arising from rerouting of local traffic to new motorway capacity were noted earlier (see section 5.4.1). This is the basis for the maxim that we cannot build our way out of congestion, which we know from experience to be generally true.

Conversely, measures to discourage certain classes of traffic, with the aim of reducing congestion, generally disappoint. These include promotion of alternative modes of travel, charging for road use and freight consolidation. Road space vacated by such measures reduces delays and so attracts back previously deterred users. A sufficiently high road user charge could reduce traffic, but such a charge would be difficult to implement politically, not least on account of concerns about inequity for low-income motorists. On the other hand, reducing carriageway available for general traffic, for instance by creating bus priority lanes, while not reducing the intensity of congestion once road users have adapted to the change, does reduce the amount of congested traffic – but this is only feasible where attractive alternative modes are available, particularly rail, which can offer a swift and reliable alternative to the car on congested roads.

Accordingly, the general intensity of congestion is difficult to reduce in populated areas or along well used routes. But there is scope for better management of road networks to achieve better outcomes for road users. While congestion results from an excess of demand over the supply of carriageway, poor traffic management can also contribute. Kurzhanskiy and Varaija (2015) have summarised US experience, where large fluctuations in delays for the same overall demand indicate poor traffic control as a cause of congestion. In London, it is estimated that three-quarters of congestion is the result of excess demand and one-quarter from planned events or unplanned incidents; 75 per cent of traffic signals continuously vary their timing to optimise flow across both individual junctions and the network as a whole, reducing junction delays by about 13 per cent. The benefits of such dynamic traffic control technology were demonstrated during the 2012 London Olympic Games, when major changes in flow were managed successfully (Emmerson 2014).

A further approach to achieving better outcomes for road users is to provide suitable travel information, as reviewed by Van Essen et al. (2016). The efficiency of use of a road network depends on individuals' behaviour, whether selfish or cooperative. Selfish choice behaviour leads to less efficient use than when individuals cooperate and make socially efficient choices. Individuals can waste up to a third of their travel time by not being cooperative. However, individuals cannot identify socially optimal outcomes for themselves, so travel information may be helpful to that end, yet much depends on how individuals respond to such information, which in turn would depend on personality attributes.

The importance of the role of travel information has been very much enhanced in recent years by the widespread adoption by road users of digital navigation (satnav), as discussed earlier (see section 2.4). There are two traffic equilibria postulated by Wardrop (1952) in his seminal paper. Wardrop's first equilibrium states that, under equilibrium conditions, traffic arranges itself in congested networks in such a way that no vehicle can reduce its costs (time and other costs) by switching routes. For this to happen in practice, drivers would need to have perfect knowledge of all feasible routes and travel times. Digital navigation may be seen as improving such knowledge, thus enhancing network efficiency, yet with a number of independent providers that may offer conflicting advice, it is hard to assess to what extent increased efficiency is being achieved.

Wardrop's first equilibrium assumes that road users make decisions without regard to the impact their choices may have on others – a 'selfish' equilibrium. According to his postulated second equilibrium, the average journey time would be at a (lesser) minimum if all users behave cooperatively in choosing their routes to ensure the most efficient use of the whole system. This would be the case if an omnipotent central authority could command them all which routes to take. Traffic flows satisfying Wardrop's second equilibrium are generally deemed system-optimal, and the loss of efficiency from this to the selfish equilibrium is an example of what is known as 'the price of anarchy' (Belov et al. 2022).

Economists argue that a more socially optimal outcome could be achieved if the costs imposed by the marginal road user on others, by adding to congestion, could be internalised by a congestion charge, thus modifying behaviour by reducing demand through higher vehicle operation costs (see section 4.8). However, implementing road pricing is difficult in practice, and there are issues of equity, so a question worthy of investigation is to what extent a more socially optimal outcome could be achieved through flexing the routing advice offered by providers of digital navigation.

The likelihood that improved operational efficiency could be achieved through digital navigation is suggested by the wide use of digital routing and navigation systems by the road freight sector (Rincon-Garcia, Waterson and Cherrett 2018). Everyday experience of online shopping indicates the use made by logistics businesses of digital technologies to manage, track and predict flows of goods, often offering delivery time slots of two hours or less, all done algorithmically. This points to techniques to achieve operational efficiency on congested road networks that might be extended to the generality of traffic in a way that could be far more cost effective and less carbon generating than civil engineering technologies.

The competing providers of digital navigation services are generally uncommunicative about their operations, while highway authorities appear to show no interest in the impact of this technology on the functioning of the road networks for which they are responsible. There is therefore likely to be scope for coordination that would improve outcomes for road users. One kind of opportunity would be when the network is under stress, for instance on the occasion of major incidents, peak holiday flows, bad weather and the like. It is probable, and certainly worth further investigation, that coordination between highway authorities and digital navigation providers could make better use of available capacity. There is also the possibility of improving operations at normal times, including avoiding routing through traffic via unsuitable minor roads.

7.4 Better modelling of road networks

The shortcomings of conventional transport modelling were discussed in Chapter 5. The advent of wide use of digital navigation opens new possibilities. While there is only fragmentary published information on how the routing algorithms function, it appears that a model of travel behaviour on the road network is constructed from trip data derived from users of the navigation service: trip origins and destinations, routes through the network, time of day/week, prevailing traffic conditions and journey times, both forecast and outturn. Such a model could be viewed as combining the trip generation, distribution and assignment stages of the standard four-stage transport model (the mode split stage not being relevant for committed road users seeking routing advice).

Many providers of digital navigation offer predictions of journey time in advance of setting out. Comparison of predicted and outturn journey times provides a check on the predictive validity of the model. Derrow-Pinion et al. (2021) have employed machine learning to improve the accuracy of journey time predictions of Google Maps by such comparison, allowing recalibration of the underlying model. This kind of check on the predictive validity is not employed for transport models generally, as discussed in section 5.3.

The type of model developed by digital navigation providers is novel and powerful in that it can utilise huge amounts of trip data, both real time and historic. A question is whether such models could be used to inform decisions on interventions aimed at improving experience on the road network. This would involve using these models for the base year description of travel behaviour on the network, and then postulating the behavioural changes resulting from the intervention. Outcomes could be monitored and compared with forecast, with discrepancies suggesting how the model could be improved. Digital navigation models already exist. Their cost of construction and operation is met by the income generated from sales, whether of direction services to business premises (as for Google Maps) or to vehicle manufacturers that fit digital navigation as standard equipment (as in the case of TomTom). So, the cost of using these models for planning purposes could be less than building and using conventional models. TomTom offers origin–destination analysis as a service and may therefore be open to suggestions for use of the underlying model for planning purposes.

Another possibility would be to create an open-source, crowd-funded digital navigation model – a kind of not-for-profit version of Waze, a provider that encourages user input. This might build on the experience of open-source journey planners used by public transport authorities, such as OpenTripPlanner or OpenStreetMap, although these do not take account of real-time traffic conditions at present. The funders might be road authorities that would gain access to the underlying model for planning purposes. A further possibility arises if some form of electronic road user charging were to be introduced, as electric propulsion replaces the internal combustion engine, to replace revenue from fuel duty (see section 6.2.3). This is likely to involve technology similar to digital navigation and might therefore be the basis of traffic modelling for other purposes.

Use of models based on digital navigation may be best suited to exploring the near-term impacts of interventions aimed at improving the experience of road users. That would be appropriate in the context of regarding the road network as substantially mature.

7.5 Economic analysis of mature networks

The main use of transport economic analysis has been to justify investment in infrastructure based on cost–benefit analysis where the main benefit is the value of travel time saving. A reorientation to regard the interurban road network as generally mature, as is the case for urban road networks, would have two main consequences for economic analysis.

First, the focus would switch to the economics of operations, closely linked to operational analysis of the network in real time, taking advantage of digital technologies that are already in wide use and are both scalable and relatively low cost compared with civil engineering technologies. Second, the remaining case for investment in infrastructure would need to be based on real observable desirable outcomes, not on notional increases in economic welfare.

The railways have substantially made this transition, in that the management of day-to-day operations has always been crucial to achieving acceptable outcomes. Besides, cost–benefit analysis has not been central to recent investment decisions: HS2, where the conventional economic case struggled to offer value for money; the integrated rail plan for the Midlands and the North, where the limitations of cost–benefit analysis were recognised; the extension of London's Northern Line to Battersea Power Station, where the decision to invest was essentially commercial; and Crossrail, where the ex-post evaluation of outcomes is unrelated to the ex-ante economic case for the investment (see section 4.16.1).

Future road investment should be justified by case-specific benefits. Increased surface access to Heathrow airport should a third runway be built was mentioned above. There may be other instances where some increase or change in location of economic activity requires additional road access, the cost of which would appropriately be funded, at least in part, by the entities benefiting. The limited evidence for general investment in the road network to boost economic growth has been noted earlier (see section 4.11). Where a major road experiences congestion during morning and evening peak flows, it must be expected that adding capacity would attract more commuting traffic diverting from other routes, with no overall economic benefit, as for the motorway-widening case studies discussed earlier (see section 5.4.1). There may also be benefits from building bypasses around town and villages, but the value of such investment needs to be justified by the value of the environmental improvement, not because the new road allows time to be saved by through traffic.

While the argument is that regarding transport networks as mature requires a focus on operations, rather than on investment in new capacity, the impact of externalities continues to be important. Yet not increasing capacity helps avoid increasing externalities related to vehicle-miles travelled, particularly tailpipe carbon and air pollutants. Road traffic congestion as an externality is largely intractable in practice, for reasons that are understood (see section 7.3 above).

7.6 Strategic case

The difficulty of articulating an economically persuasive strategic case for a programme of transport investment was discussed earlier (see section 4.17). Regarding the transport system as substantially mature changes the main challenge from justifying a collection of investment projects to reconciling transport operations with the Net Zero objective. The key elements of a strategy, whether of a particular sector or of transport provision as a whole, are: the switch to zero-emission vehicles for surface transport; employment of digital technologies to optimise network operations; and financial support for public transport; with investment in new capacity justified case by case to support economic development, such decisions taken jointly with planners and developers, and schemes funded in part by developers.

Strategic thinking about transport provision would be facilitated by devolution of budgets to cities and their surrounding regions, where decisions can be taken that relate transport to land use, economic development and demographic change, treating transport as a demand derived from granular consideration and local knowledge of such developments, rather than based on central guidance and historic econometric parameters.

Aviation is different from surface transport and more difficult, however, given the lack of near-term alternatives to substantial dependence on oil-based kerosene. The most straightforward approach would be to cap airport capacity, as discussed earlier (see section 4.16.3), while facilitating the deployment of carbon-free technologies, fostered by mandates for increasing minimum usage of alternative fuels over time.

7.7 Conclusions

The era of growth of travel based on the energy of fossil fuels began in the early nineteenth century with the coming of the railways and ended at the close of the twentieth century, when per capita travel demand in developed economies ceased to increase. The current era is characterised by the need to decarbonise the transport sector, largely by switching to electric propulsion. Significant reduction in per capita travel demand is unlikely since we have become habituated to high levels of access to people, places, activities and services within built environments that are slow to change. Accordingly, the main means of decarbonisation involve technological change, not behavioural change. Yet the cessation of demand growth seen since the turn of the century has been a helpful and timely change in travel behaviour, the consequence of both the saturation of demand for travel and the lack of technologies to permit faster travel within constrained travel time.

The shift, from an era of growth of travel demand to one of cessation of growth, now needs to be paralleled by a shift from investment in additional transport capacity to making best use of existing assets, which avoids exacerbating transport-sector carbon emissions. The key technological developments are electric propulsion for vehicles and the associated electric charging provision, plus the deployment of digital technologies to improve the operational efficiency of road and rail networks.

The related changes to analytical methodologies involve a paradigm shift from the economic appraisal and modelling of additional capacity to the analysis of operations. For roads in particular, there has been a gulf that needs to be bridged between the relevant disciplines: between economic analysis of transport investment and of operations; and between civil engineering and operations research. For the road system, analysis and modelling of operations has been very largely neglected, as seen by omission of this topic from the thousand pages of the UK Department for Transport's Transport Analysis Guidance. Fresh thinking is needed.

The main directions for fresh thinking about travel behaviour, the subject of this book, and the associated investment in the transport system, its economic analysis and modelling, comprise the following:

- Rethink transport investment analysis and modelling to reflect observed travel behaviour, saving time in the short run but gaining increased access in the longer run.
- Recognise that access is subject to diminishing returns, so that transport systems tend to maturity, with stable per capita travel behaviour. This implies investment priority be given to maintain and renew capital assets, as well as to exploit digital technologies to make better use of assets.
- New transport technologies are unlikely to increase access significantly, so their uptake will depend on the journey quality benefits for which users are willing to pay. Adoption of electric propulsion is driven by regulation in response to climate change.
- The benefits of any proposed investment in new capacity need to be justified by the value of the projected observable outcomes, which will generally involve changes in land use.
- Congestion is largely an intractable problem, not alleviated by road capacity expansion or road pricing with likely publicly acceptable charges. The best means for mitigating the perceived impact is digital navigation, which needs to be recognised by road authorities.
- Climate change is the prime strategic challenge for the transport sector. The main response is electrification of vehicles, facilitated by investment in charging points. Behaviour change, in particular to reduce car use beyond city centres, is difficult to achieve, yet efforts to do so are warranted.

These topics comprise an agenda for practitioners and policymakers, as well as for researchers wishing to advance applicable understanding of the complex system of travel and transport.

References

Acheampong, R. and Silva, E. 2015. 'Land-use transport interaction modelling: A review of the literature and future research directions'. *Journal of Transport and Land Use* 8(3): 11–38.

Ahmed, A. and Stopher, P. 2014. 'Seventy minutes plus or minus 10: A review of travel time budget studies'. *Transport Reviews* 34(5): 607–25.

Airports Commission. 2015. *Airports Commission: Final report*. London: Airports Commission.

Aksoy, C., Barrero, J., Bloom, N., Davis, S., Dolls, M. and Zarate, P. 2023. *Working from Home around the Globe: 2023 Report*. https://www.econpol.eu/sites/default/files/2023-07/EconPol-PolicyBrief_53.pdf. Accessed 16 February 2024.

Alonso, W. 1964. *Location and Land Use: Towards a general theory of land rent*. Cambridge, MA: Harvard University Press.

Anable, J., Brown, L., Docherty, I. and Marsden, G. 2022. *Less Is More: Changing travel in a post-pandemic society*. Oxford: Centre for Research into Energy Demand Solutions.

Arnott, B., Rehackova, L., Errington, L., Sniehotta, F., Roberts, J. and Araujo-Soares, V. 2014. 'Efficacy of behavioural interventions for transport behaviour change: Systematic review, meta-analysis and intervention coding'. *International Journal of Behavioural Nutrition and Physical Activity* 11: Article 133.

Arup. 2016. *Research into the Appraisal of Long Term Benefits of Transport Schemes: Final report*. London: Arup.

Arup. 2019. *Programmatic Appraisal: Stage 5 report*. London: Arup.

Arup. 2022. *Evaluation of Crossrail Pre-Opening Property Impacts*. London: Transport for London and Department for Transport.

Atkins. 2019. *NTM Future Development Quality Report [for the Department for Transport]*. Epsom: Atkins.

Avineri, E. 2012. 'On the use and potential of behavioural economics from the perspective of transport and climate change'. *Journal of Transport Geography* 24: 512–21.

Bain, R. 2009. 'Error and optimism bias in toll road traffic forecasts'. *Transportation* 36: 469–82.

Baldwin, A. and Shuttleworth, K. 2021. *How Governments Use Evidence to Make Transport Policy*. London: Institute for Government.

Banister, D. 2018. *Inequality in Transport*. Abingdon: Alexandrine Press.

Banister, D. and Thurstain-Goodwin, M. 2011. 'Quantification of the non-transport benefits resulting from rail investment'. *Journal of Transport Geography* 19: 212–23.

Barrero, J., Bloom, N. and Davis, S. 2023. 'The evolution of work from home'. *Journal of Economic Perspectives* 37(4): 23–50.

Batley, R., Bates, J., Bliemer, M. et al. 2019. 'New appraisal values of travel time saving and reliability in Great Britain'. *Transportation* 46(3): 583–621.

Batley, R., Dekker, T. and Mackie, P. 2022. *Congested Values of Travel Time (CVTT): Re-analysis of the 2014/15 SP study*. Leeds: Institute of Transport Studies.

Batty, M. 2015. 'Models again: Their role in planning and prediction'. *Environment and Planning B* 42(2): 191–4.

Bauer, P., Thorpe, A. and Brunet, G. 2015. 'The quiet revolution of numerical weather prediction'. *Nature* 525: 47–55.

Beck, M., Hess, S., Cabral, M. and Dubernet, I. 2017. 'Valuing travel time savings: A case of short-term or long-term choices?'. *Transportation Research Part E* 100: 133–43.

Belov, A., Mattas, K., Makridis, M., Menendez, M. and Ciuffo, B. 2022. 'A microsimulation based analysis of the price of anarchy in traffic routing: The enhanced Braess network case'. *Journal of Intelligent Transportation Systems* 26(4): 448–60.

Blagden, J. and Tanner, W. 2021. *Network Effects: Why levelling up demands a new approach to connectivity*. London: Onward.

BloombergNEF. 2023. *Electric Vehicle Outlook 2023*. Bloomberg Finance.

Börjesson, M., Kouwenhoven, M., de Jong, G. and Daly, A. 2023. 'Can repeated surveys reveal the variation of the value of travel time over time?'. *Transportation* 50: 245–84.

Boyce, D. and Williams, H. 2015. *Forecasting Urban Travel: Past, present and future*. Cheltenham: Edward Elgar.

Buchanan, P. 2018. *The Appraisal and Business Case for Crossrail*. London: Crossrail Learning Legacy.

Buehler, R., Pucher, J., Gerike, R. and Gotschi, T. 2017. 'Reducing car dependence in the heart of Europe: Lessons from Germany, Austria, and Switzerland'. *Transport Reviews* 37(1): 4–28.

Cairncross, F. 1997. *The Death of Distance*. Boston, MA: Harvard Business School Press.

Caltrans. 2020. *Transport Analysis Framework: Evaluating transportation impacts of state highway system projects*. Sacramento: California Department of Transportation.

Centre for Cities. 2022. *Cities Outlook 2022*. London: Centre for Cities.

CEPA. 2023. *Transformative Impacts of Transport Investment: Case study report for the Department for Transport*. London: Cambridge Economic Policy Associates.

Chatterjee, K., Goodwin, P., Schwanen, T. et al. 2018. *Young People's Travel: What's changed and why? Review and analysis: Report to Department for Transport*. Bristol: University of the West of England.

Chatterjee, K. et al. 2019. *Access to Transport and Life Opportunities: Report to the Department for Transport*. London: NatCen Social Research.

City of Copenhagen 2019. *Copenhagen City of Cyclists: The bicycle account 2018*. City of Copenhagen.

Clark, B. and Parkin, J. 2022. *Cycling Diversion Factors: Rapid evidence assessment summary report to Department for Transport*. Bristol: University of the West of England.

Climate Change Committee. 2020. *The Sixth Carbon Budget: Surface transport*. London: Climate Change Committee.

Climate Change Committee. 2023. *Progress in Reducing Emissions: 2023 report to Parliament*. London: Climate Change Committee.

Corlett, A. and Marshall, J. 2023. *Where the Rubber Hits the Road: Reforming vehicle taxes*. London: Resolution Foundation.

Coyle, D. 2022. 'Shaping successful mega-project investments'. *Oxford Review of Economic Policy* 38(2): 224–36.

Coyle, D. and Sensier, M. 2022. 'The imperial treasury: Appraisal methodology and regional economic performance in the UK'. *Regional Studies* 54(3): 283–95.

Cruz, C. and Sarmento, J. 2019. 'Traffic forecast inaccuracy in transportation: A literature review of roads and railway projects'. *Transportation* 47: 1571–1606.

Currie, G. and Fournier, N. 2020. 'Why most DRT/Micro-Transits fail: What the survivors tell us about progress'. *Research in Transportation Economics* 83: 100895.

Dale, S., Frost, M., Ison, S. and Budd, L. 2019. 'The impact of the Nottingham workplace parking levy on travel to work mode share'. *Case Studies on Transport Policy* 7(4): 749–60.

Daly, A. 2021. 'Loss aversion and size and time effects in value of time studies'. In Roger Vickerman (ed.), *International Encyclopedia of Transportation* 1: 165–9. Amsterdam: Elsevier.

Daly, A. and Hess, S. 2020. 'VTT or VTTS: A note on terminology for value of travel time work'. *Transportation* 47: 1359–64.

Daly, A., Tsang, F. and Rohr, C. 2014. 'The value of small time savings for non-business travel'. *Journal of Transport Economics and Policy* 48(2): 205–18.

Dam, D., Melcangi, D, Pilossoph, L. and Toner-Rodgers, A. 2022. 'What have workers done with the time freed up by commuting less?'. *Liberty Street Economics*, 18 October.

DBEIS. 2021. *Valuation of Greenhouse Gas Emissions: For policy appraisal and evaluation*. London: Department for Business, Energy & Industrial Strategy.

DCLG. 2017. *Housing Infrastructure Fund: Supporting document for forward funding*. London: Department of Communities and Local Government.

Derrow-Pinion, A. et al. 2021. 'ETA prediction with graph neural networks in Google Maps'. arXiv:2108.11482.

DfT. 2005. *Transport, Wider Economic Benefits, and Impacts on GDP: Discussion paper*. London: Department for Transport.

DfT. 2009. *Low Carbon Transport: A greener future*. London: Department for Transport.

DfT. 2015. *Review of Airports Commission's Final Report*. London: Department for Transport.

DfT. 2016a. *Evaluation of Concessionary Bus Travel: The impacts of the free bus pass*. London: Department for Transport.

DfT. 2016b. *Strengthening the Links between Appraisal and Evaluation*. London: Department for Transport.

DfT. 2018a. *Capturing Housing Impacts in Transport Appraisal: Case studies*. London: Department for Transport.

DfT 2018b. *Road Traffic Forecasts 2018*. London: Department for Transport.

DfT 2019a. *Transport and Technology: Public attitudes tracker: Wave 4 summary report*. London: Department for Transport.

DfT. 2019b. *Appraisal and Modelling Strategy: Informing future investment decisions*. London: Department for Transport.

DfT. 2020a. *Full Business Case: High Speed 2 phase 1*. London: Department for Transport.

DfT 2020b. *National Transport Model: Analytical review*. London: Department for Transport.

DfT. 2021a. *Integrated Rail Plan for the North and the Midlands CP490*. London: Department for Transport.

DfT. 2021b. *Appraisal and Modelling Strategy: TAG update report*. London: Department for Transport.

DfT 2021c. *Planning Ahead for the Strategic Road Network: Developing the Third Road Investment Strategy*. London: Department for Transport.

DfT. 2021d. *Capturing Local Context in Transport Appraisal: Case studies*. London: Department for Transport.

DfT. 2021e. *Decarbonising Transport: A better, greener Britain*. London: Department for Transport.

DfT. 2022a. *Transport Business Case Guidance*. London: Department for Transport.

DfT. 2022b. *National Road Traffic Projections 2022*. London: Department for Transport.

DfT. 2023a. *Zero Emission Vehicle (ZEV) Mandate Consultation: Summary of responses and joint government response*. London: Department for Transport.

DfT. 2023b. *Zero Emissions Vehicle Mandate and Non-ZEV Efficiency Requirements: Consultation-stage cost benefit analysis*. London: Department for Transport.

DfT. 2023c. *Draft National Policy Statement for National Networks*. London: Department for Transport

DfT. 2023d. *Government Response to Developing a UK Sustainable Aviation Fuel Industry Report*. London: Department for Transport.

DfT. 2023e. *Domestic Transport Use by Mode*. London: Department for Transport.

DfT. 2023f. *Cycle Index, England*. London: Department for Transport.

DLUHC. 2023. *DLUHC Appraisal Guide*. London: Department for Levelling Up, Housing and Communities.

Docherty, I. and Waite, D. 2018. *Evidence Review: Infrastructure PIN – 03*. Glasgow: Productivity Insights Network.

Downs, A. 1962. 'The law of peak-hour expressway congestion'. *Traffic Quarterly*, July: 393–409.

Dunkerley, F., Rohr, C. and Wardman, M. 2021. 'Elasticities for travel demand: Recent evidence'. In Roger Vickerman (ed.), *International Encyclopedia of Transportation* 1: 179–84. Amsterdam: Elsevier.

Duranton, G. and Guerra, E. 2016. *Developing a Common Narrative on Urban Accessibility: An urban planning perspective*. Washington, DC: Brookings Institution.

Duranton, G. and Puga, D. 2015. 'Urban land use'. In G. Duranton, V. Henderson and W. Strange (eds), *Handbook of Regional and Urban Economics*. Amsterdam: Elsevier.

Duranton, G. and Turner, M. 2011. 'The fundamental law of road congestion: Evidence from US cities'. *American Economic Review* 101: 2616–52.

Eliasson, J. 2017. 'Is congestion pricing fair? Consumer and citizen perspectives on equity effects'. In *Income Inequality, Social Inclusion and Mobility: Round table report*, 165–92. Paris: International Transport Forum, OECD Publishing.

Emmerson, G. 2014. 'Maximising use of the road network in London'. In S. Glaister and E. Box (eds), *Moving Cities: The future of urban travel*. London: RAC Foundation.

Erhardt, G., Hoque, J, Chen, M. et al. 2020. *Traffic Forecasting Accuracy Assessment Research*. Washington, DC: National Academies Press.

Faraday Institution. 2023. *The Role of Hydrogen and Batteries in Delivering Net Zero in the UK by 2050*. Didcot: Faraday Institution.

Flyvbjerg, B. 2007. 'Cost overruns and demand shortfalls in urban rail and other infrastructure'. *Transportation Planning and Technology* 30(1): 9–30.

Flyvbjerg, B. 2008. 'Curbing optimism bias and strategic misrepresentation in planning: Reference class forecasting in practice'. *European Planning Studies* 16(1): 3–21.

Fosgerau, M. and Pilegaard, N. 2021. 'The rule-of-a-half and interpreting the consumer surplus as accessibility'. In Roger Vickerman (ed.), *International Encyclopedia of Transportation* 1: 237–41. Amsterdam: Elsevier.

Frontier Economics. 2022. *Economic Research on the Impact of Carbon Pricing on the UK Aviation Sector: Final report.* London: Frontier Economics with Air Transportation Analytics.

Garcia-López, M., Pasidis, I. and Viladecans-Marsal, E. 2022. 'Congestion in highways when tolls and railroads matter: Evidence from European cities'. *Journal of Economic Geography* 22(5): 931–60.

Gatersleben, B. 2021. 'Social-symbolic and affective aspects of car ownership and use'. In Roger Vickerman (ed.), *International Encyclopedia of Transportation* 7: 81–5. Amsterdam: Elsevier.

Gates, S., Gogescu, F., Grollman, G., Cooper, E. and Khambhaita, P. 2019. *Transport and Inequality: An evidence review for the Department for Transport.* London: National Centre for Social Research.

Geurs, K. and Van Wee, B. 2004. 'Accessibility evaluation of land-use and transport strategies: Review and research directions'. *Journal of Transport Geography* 12(2): 127–40.

Geurs, K., Zondag, B., de Jong, G. and de Bok, M. 2010. 'Accessibility appraisal of land-use/transport policy strategies: More than just adding up travel-time savings'. *Transportation Research Part D* 15(7): 382–93.

Gibbons, S. 2017. *Planes, Trains and Automobiles: The economic impact of transport infrastructure.* Spatial Economics Research Centre Policy Paper 13. London: London School of Economics.

Gibbons, S. and Machin, S. 2005. 'Valuing rail access using transport innovations'. *Journal of Urban Economics* 57(1): 148–69.

Gilmour, D. and Flynn, S. 2020. *Who Uses the M25?* Presentation to the RAC Foundation. https://www.racfoundation.org/data-driven/who-uses-the-m25. Accessed 16 February 2024.

Glaister, S. 2018. 'The Smeed Report at 50: Will road pricing always be 10 years away?'. In John Walker (ed.), *Road Pricing: Technologies, economics and acceptability.* London: Institute of Engineering and Technology.

Glaister, S. 2021. *HS2: Levelling up or the pursuit of an icon?* London: Institute for Government.

Gonzales-Pampillon, N. and Overman, H. 2020. *Regional Differences in UK Transport BCRs: An empirical assessment.* Centre for Economic Performance, occasional paper 53. London: London School of Economics.

Goodwin, P. 1995. 'Car dependence'. *Transport Policy* 2(3): 151–2.

Goodwin, P. 1996. 'Empirical evidence on induced traffic'. *Transportation* 23(1): 35–54.

Goodwin, P. 2019. 'Forecasting road traffic and its significance for transport policy'. In I. Docherty and D. Shaw (eds), *Transport Matters*, 153–76. Bristol: Policy Press.

Goodwin, P. and Van Dender, K. 2013. '"Peak car": Themes and issues'. *Transport Reviews* 33(3): 243–54.

Graham, A. and Metz, D. 2017. 'Limits to air travel growth: The case of infrequent flyers'. *Journal of Air Transport Management* 62: 109–20.

Graver, B. et al. 2022. *Vision 2050: Aligning aviation with the Paris Agreement.* Washington, DC: International Council on Clean Transportation.

Grimes, A. and Liang, Y. 2010. 'Bridge to somewhere: Valuing Auckland's northern motorway extensions'. *Journal of Transport Economics and Policy* 44(3): 287–315.

Guan, X., Wang, D. and Cao, X. 2020. 'The role of residential self-selection in land use-travel research: A review of recent findings'. *Transport Reviews* 40(3): 267–87.

Halket, J., Mysliwski, M., Nesheim, L. and Simpson, P. 2019. *Property Value Uplift Tool: Final report.* London: Institute for Fiscal Studies.

Hall, M., Van Vliet, D. and Willumsen, L. 1980. 'SATURN: A simulation-assignment model for the evaluation of traffic management schemes'. *Traffic Engineering & Control* 21: 168–76.

Handy, S. 2020. 'Is accessibility an idea whose time has finally come?'. *Transportation Research Part D* 83: 102319.

Hartgen, D. 2013. 'Hubris or humility? Accuracy issues for the next 50 years of travel demand modeling'. *Transportation* 40: 1133–57.

Helm, D. 2023. 'Net zero electricity: The UK 2035 target'. *Oxford Review of Economic Policy* 39(4): 779–95.

Hensher, D., Rose, J., Ortuzar, J. and Rizzi, L. 2009. 'Estimating the willingness to pay and value of risk reduction for car occupants in the road environment'. *Transportation Research Part A* 43(7): 692–707.

Hess, S., Daly, D. and Börjesson, M. 2020. 'A critical appraisal of the use of simple time-money trade-offs for appraisal value of travel time measures'. *Transportation* 47(3): 1541–70.

Hickman, R. and Dean, M. 2018. 'Incomplete cost-benefit analysis in transport appraisal'. *Transport Reviews* 38(6): 689–709.

Higgins, C. and Kanaroglou, P. 2016. 'Forty years of modelling rapid transit's land value uplift in North America: Moving beyond the tip of the iceberg'. *Transport Reviews* 36(5): 610–34.

Highways Agency. 2011. *Post Opening Project Evaluation of Major Schemes (2002–2009): Meta-analysis main report*. London: Highways Agency.

Highways England. 2016. *Post Opening Project Evaluation of Major Schemes: Meta-analysis 2015*. London: Highways England.

Highways England. 2017. *A303 Stonehenge Amesbury to Berwick Down: Valuing heritage impacts*. London: Highways England. https://infrastructure.planninginspectorate.gov.uk/wp-content/ipc/uploads/projects/TR010025/TR010025-001183-Highways%20England%20-%20Contingent%20Valuation%20Survey.pdf. Accessed 16 February 2024.

Highways England. 2018. *A303 Amesbury to Berwick Down TR010024: 7.5 Combined modelling and appraisal report*. London: Highways England. https://infrastructure.planninginspectorate.gov.uk/wp-content/ipc/uploads/projects/TR010025/TR010025-000451-7-5-ComMA.pdf. Accessed 16 February 2024.

Hirsch, F. 1977. *Social Limits to Growth*. London: Routledge and Kegan Paul.

Hive IT. 2020. *Department for Transport: NTEM discovery report*. Sheffield: Hive IT.

HM Government. 2023. *Carbon Budget Delivery Plan. HC1269*. London: House of Commons.

HMT. 2020. *Green Book Review 2020: Findings and response*. London: HM Treasury.

HMT. 2022. *The Green Book (2022)*. London: HM Treasury.

Hollander, Y. 2016. *Transport Modelling for a Complete Beginner*. London: CTthink.

House of Commons Transport Committee. 2023. *Road Pricing: Government response to the Committee's fourth report of session 2021–22, Appendix 2, HC1178*. London: House of Commons.

HS2. 2013. *London–West Midlands Environmental Statement, Volume 3: Route-wide effects*. London: High Speed Two (HS2) Limited.

HS2. 2023. *PLANET Framework Model PFMv10a: Model description report*. Birmingham: High Speed Two (HS2) Limited.

International Council on Clean Transportation. 2020. *Vision 2050: A strategy to decarbonize the global transport sector by mid-century*. Washington, DC: International Council on Clean Transportation.

International Energy Agency. 2021. *Global SUV Sales: Commentary 21 December*. Paris: International Energy Agency.

ITF. 2017. *Linking People and Places: New ways of understanding spatial access in cities*. Paris: International Transport Forum, OECD Publishing.

ITF. 2019. *What is the Value of Saving Travel Time?* International Transport Forum Roundtable Reports, no. 176. Paris: International Transport Forum, OECD Publishing.

ITF. 2020. *Accessibility and Transport Appraisal: Summary and conclusions*. International Transport Forum Roundtable Reports, no. 182. Paris: OECD Publishing.

ITF. 2021. *Reversing Car Dependency: Summary and conclusions*. International Transport Forum Roundtable Reports, no. 181. Paris: OECD Publishing.

ITF. 2022. *Broadening Transport Appraisal*. Paris: International Transport Forum, OECD Publishing.

ITF. 2023. *Shaping Post-Covid Mobility in Cities: Summary and conclusions*. International Transport Forum Roundtable Reports, no. 190. Paris: OECD Publishing.

Jara-Diaz, S. 2007. *Transport Economic Theory*. Bingley: Emerald Group Publishing.

Jones, P., Eyers, T., Bray, J., Georgeson, N., Powell, T., Paris, J. and Lane, R. 2004. *The Jubilee Line Extension Study: Main findings and lessons learned*. Paper presented to the European Transport Conference, Strasbourg, France.

Jones, P. 2018. *Urban Mobility: Preparing for the future, learning from the past. CREATE project summary and recommendations*. https://create-mobility.eu/RESOURCES/MATERIAL/CREATE-ProjectSummaryReccommendations.pdf. Accessed 16 February 2024.

JTS. 2017. *Journey Time Statistics*. London: Department for Transport.

Kallbekken, S. and Victor, D. 2022. 'A cleaner future for flight: Aviation needs a radical redesign'. *Nature* 609: 673–5.

Kay, J. 2010. *Obliquity: Why our goals are best achieved indirectly*. London: Profile.

Knowles, R. and Ferbrache, F. 2016. 'Evaluation of the wider impact of light rail investment on cities'. *Journal of Transport Geography* 54: 430–9.

Kodukula, S., Rudolph, F., Jansen, U. and Amon, E. 2018. *Living. Moving. Breathing*. Wuppertal: Wuppertal Institute.

Kurzhanskiy, A. and Varaija, P. 2015. 'Traffic management: An outlook'. *Economics of Transportation* 4(3): 135–46.

Ladd, B. 2012. '"You can't build your way out of congestion." – Or can you?'. *disP: The Planning Review* 48(3): 16–23.

Laird, J. and Johnson, D. 2021. 'The GDP effects of transport investments: The macroeconomic approach'. In Roger Vickerman (ed.), *International Encyclopedia of Transportation* 1: 256–62. Amsterdam: Elsevier.

Laird, J. and Venables, A. 2017. 'Transport investment and economic performance: A framework for economic appraisal'. *Transport Policy* 56: 1–11.

Lam, D. and Wengraf, I. 2023. *Is It Necessary to Reduce Car Mileage to Meet Our Carbon Emission Goals?* London: RAC Foundation.

Lee, H., Lim, W. and Leong, W. 2018. 'Land enhancement and intensification benefits of investing in an urban rail network'. *Research in Transportation Economics* 69: 512–22.

Leunig, T. 2011. *Cart or Horse: Transport and economic growth*. International Transport Forum Discussion Paper 2011-4. Paris: OECD Publishing.

Le Vine, S. and White, P. 2020. *The Shape of Changing Bus Demand in England*. London: Independent Transport Commission.

Levinson, D. 2014. 'Extrapolations in traffic vs. reality.' *Transportist*, 3 December. https://transportist.org/2014/12/03/extrapolations-in-traffic-vs-reality. Accessed 16 February 2024.

Li, P. and Strachan, N. 2021. *Energy Modelling in the UK: Decision making in government and industry*. London: UK Energy Research Centre.

Litman, T. 2022. *Generated Traffic and Induced Traffic: Implications for transport planning*. Victoria, BC: Victoria Transport Policy Institute. https://www.vtpi.org/gentraf.pdf. Accessed 16 February 2024.

Long, A., Carney, F. and Kandt, J. 2023. 'Who is returning to public transport for non-work trips after COVID-19? Evidence from older citizens' smart cards in the UK's second largest city region'. *Journal of Transport Geography* 107: 103529.

Lyons, G. 2002. 'Internet: Investigating new technology's evolving role, nature and effects on transport'. *Transport Policy* 9(4): 335–46.

Mackie, P., Batley, R. and Worsley, T. 2018. 'Valuing transport investments based on travel time savings: A response to David Metz'. *Case Studies on Transport Policy* 6(4): 638–41.

Mackie, P., Worsley, T. and Eliasson, J. 2014. 'Transport appraisal revisited'. *Research in Transport Economics* 47: 3–18.

Manville, M., Taylor, B. D., Blumenberg, E. and Schouten, A. 2023. 'Vehicle access and falling transit ridership: Evidence from Southern California'. *Transportation* 50: 303–29.

Marsden, G. 2023. *Reverse Gear: The reality and implications of national transport emission reduction policies*. Oxford: Centre for Research into Energy Demand Solutions.

Marshall, W. and Dumbaugh, E. 2020. 'Revisiting the relationship between traffic congestion and the economy: A longitudinal examination of US metropolitan areas'. *Transportation* 47: 275–314.

Marshall, B., Rigby, C., Haywood, A., Sheerin, C. and Behailu, A. 2023. *Our Changing Travel: Research into how people's travel choices are changing, November 2022*. London: Ipsos.

Marchetti, C. 1994. 'Anthropological invariants in travel behaviour'. *Technological Forecasting and Social Change* 47: 75–88.

Medda, F. 2012. 'Land value capture finance for transport accessibility: A review'. *Journal of Transport Geography* 25: 154–61.

Mejía Dorantes, L. and Murauskaite-Bull, I. 2022. *Transport Poverty: A systematic literature review in Europe*. Luxembourg: Publications Office of the European Union.

Metcalf, R. and Dolan, P. 2012. 'Behavioural economics and its implications for transport'. *Journal of Transport Geography* 24: 503–11.

Metz, D. 2005. 'Journey quality as the focus of future transport policy'. *Transport Policy* 12 (4): 353–9.

Metz, D. 2006. 'Accidents overvalued in road scheme appraisal'. *Proceedings of the Institution of Civil Engineers: Transport* 159(4): 159–63.

Metz, D. 2008. 'The myth of travel time saving'. *Transport Reviews* 28(3): 321–36.

Metz, D. 2010. 'Saturation of demand for daily travel'. *Transport Reviews* 30(5): 659–74.

Metz, D. 2013a. 'Mobility, access and choice: A new source of evidence'. *Journal of Transport and Land Use* 6(2): 1–4.

Metz, D. 2013b. 'Peak car and beyond: The fourth era of travel'. *Transport Reviews* 33(3): 255–70.

Metz, D. 2017. 'Valuing transport investments based on travel time savings: Inconsistency with United Kingdom policy objectives'. *Case Studies on Transport Policy* 5(4): 716–21.

Metz, D. 2018. 'Tackling urban traffic congestion: The experience of London, Stockholm and Singapore'. *Case Studies on Transport Policy* 6(4): 494–8.

Metz, D. 2019. *Driving Change: Travel in the Twenty-First Century*. Newcastle upon Tyne: Agenda.

Metz, D. 2021a. 'Time constraints and travel behaviour'. *Transportation Planning and Technology* 44(1): 16–29.

Metz, D. 2021b. 'Economic benefits of road widening: Discrepancy between outturn and forecast'. *Transportation Research Part A* 147: 312–19.

Metz, D. 2021c. 'Plateau car'. In Roger Vickerman (ed.), *International Encyclopedia of Transportation* 6: 324–30. Amsterdam: Elsevier.

Metz, D. 2022a. *Good to Go? Decarbonising travel after the pandemic.* London: London Publishing Partnership.

Metz, D. 2022b. 'The impact of digital navigation on travel behaviour'. *UCL Open Environment* 4. DOI: 10.14324/111.444/ucloe.000034.

Metz, D. 2023a. 'Drivers' perspectives of car dependence'. *Urban Planning* 8(3): 125–34.

Metz, D. 2023b. 'Digital navigation negates the economic benefits of road widening: The case of the M1 motorway'. *Transportation Research Part A* 174: 103749.

Michie, S., Van Stralen, M. and West, R. 2011. 'The behaviour change wheel: A new method for characterising and designing behaviour change interventions'. *Implementation Science* 6: Article 42.

MIT. 2019. *MIT Energy Initiative 2019: Insights into future mobility, section 3.4.* Cambridge, MA: MIT Energy Initiative. http://energy.mit.edu/insights-into-future-mobility. Accessed 16 February 2024.

Mitchell, K. 2018. 'An analysis of long-term trends in travel patterns'. In *Analyses from the National Travel Survey*. London: Department for Transport.

Mohammad, S., Graham, D., Melo, P. and Anderson, R. 2013. 'A meta-analysis of the impact of rail projects on land and property values'. *Transportation Research Part A* 50: 158–70.

Mokhtarian, P. and Chen, C. 2004. 'TTB or not TTB, that is the question: A review of the empirical literature on travel time (and money) budgets'. *Transportation Research Part A* 38(9–10): 643–75.

Mokhtarian, P., Salomon, I. and Singer, M. 2015. 'What moves us? An interdisciplinary exploration of reasons for traveling'. *Transport Reviews* 35(3): 250–74.

Moody, J., Farr, E., Papagelis, M. and Keith, D. 2021. 'The value of car ownership and use in the United States'. *Nature Sustainability* 4: 769–74.

Moody, J. and Zhao, J. 2019. 'Car pride and its bidirectional relations with car ownership: Case studies in New York City and Houston'. *Transportation Research Part A* 124: 334–53.

MoT. 1964. *Road Pricing: The economic and technical possibilities*. London: Ministry of Transport.

Morgan, M., Morton, C., Monsuur, F., Lovelace, R. and Heinen, E. 2022. *Understanding Change in Car Use over Time (UnCCUT): End of project report*. Leeds: DecarboN8.

NAO. 2019. *Improving the A303 between Amesbury and Berwick Down*. London: National Audit Office.

Nellthorp, J. 2017. 'The principles behind transport appraisal'. In Jonathon Cowie and Stephen Ison (eds), *The Routledge Handbook of Transport Economics*, 176–208. Abingdon: Routledge.

Nellthorp, J., Ojeda Cabral, M., Johnson, D., Leahy, C. and Jiang, L. 2019. *Land Value and Transport (Phase 2): Modelling and appraisal. Final report to TfN, WYCA and EPSRC*. Leeds: Institute for Transport Studies, University of Leeds.

Network Rail. 2018. *Digital Railway Strategy*. London: Network Rail.

Network Rail. 2020. *Traction Decarbonisation Network Strategy: Interim programme business case*. London: Network Rail.

New Economics Foundation. 2018. *Flying Low: The true cost of Heathrow's new runway*. London: New Economics Foundation.

Newman, P. and Kenworthy, J. 2011. '"Peak car use": Understanding the demise of automobile dependence'. *World Transport Policy and Practice* 17(2): 31–9.

NIC. 2019. *Capturing the Value of Urban Transport Investments*. London: National Infrastructure Commission.

NIC. 2020. *Rail Needs Assessment for the Midlands and the North: Final report*. London: National Infrastructure Commission.

NIC. 2021. *The Long Term Role of Cars in Towns*. London: National Infrastructure Commission.

Noland, R. and Lem, L. 2002. 'A review of the evidence for induced travel and changes in transportation and environmental policy in the US and the UK'. *Transportation Research Part D* 7(1): 1–26.

NTS [various dates]. *National Travel Survey*. London: Department for Transport.

OBR. 2023. *Emissions and our Tax Forecasts*. Working paper no. 18. London: Office for Budget Responsibility.

Ojeda-Cabral, M., Hess, S. and Batley, R. 2018. 'Understanding valuation of travel time changes: Are preferences different under different stated choice design settings?'. *Transportation* 45: 1–21.

ONS. 2021. *How People with a Vaccine Spent Their Time – one year on from the first UK lockdown: Great Britain March 2021*. Fareham: Office for National Statistics.

ONS. 2023a. *Characteristics of Homeworkers, Great Britain: September 2022 to January 2023*. Fareham: Office for National Statistics.

ONS. 2023b. *Internet Sales as a Percentage of Total Retail Sales*. Fareham: Office for National Statistics

ONS. 2024. *2021-Based Interim National Population Projections*. Fareham: Office for National Statistics.

ORR. 2022. *Rail Infrastructure and Assets, April 2021 to March 2022*. London: Office of Rail and Road.

Ortuzar, J. and Willumsen, L. 2011. *Modelling Transport*, fourth edition. Chichester: Wiley.

Osenton, T. 2004. *The Death of Demand*. Upper Saddle River, NJ: Financial Times/Prentice Hall.

Oxford Global Projects. 2020. *Updating the Evidence behind the Optimism Bias Uplifts for Transport Appraisals*. London: Department for Transport.

Plötz, P., Link, S., Ringelschwendner, H. et al. 2022. *Real-World Usage of Plug-In Hybrid Vehicles in Europe: A 2022 update on fuel consumption, electric driving and CO_2 emissions*. Berlin: International Council on Clean Transportation Europe.

Porter, C. 2014. *Northern Line Extension to Battersea: Infrastructure investment to enable development and land use change*. Frankfurt: European Transport Conference.

Preston, J. 2023. '"All things must pass": Recent changes to competition and ownership of public transport in Great Britain'. *Research in Transportation Economics* 99: 101281.

Proost, S. and Thisse, J-F. 2019. 'What can be learned from spatial economics?'. *Journal of Economic Literature* 57(3): 575–643.

Public Health England. 2020. *Achieving Behaviour Change: A guide for national government*. London: Public Health England.

PwC. 2014. *Economy: Wider impacts assessment*. London: PwC for Airports Commission.

PwC. 2022. *Wider Economic Assessment with a S-CGE model [for HS2 High Speed 2 (HS2) Limited]*. London: PwC for Department for Transport.

Quinio. 2022. *What Can We Learn from Germany's €9-a-Month Public Transport Scheme?* London: Centre for Cities.

RAC Foundation. 2017. *Using Behaviour Changes Techniques: Guidance for the road safety community*. London: RAC Foundation.

Ricardo. 2021. *Lifecycle Analysis of UK Road Vehicles*. Harwell: Ricardo Energy and Environment.

Ricardo. 2023. *Measurement of Emissions from Brake and Tyre Wear: Final report phase 1*. Harwell: Ricardo Energy and Environment.

Rincon-Garcia, N. Waterson, B. and Cherrett, T. 2018. 'Requirements from vehicle routing software: Perspectives from literature, developers and the freight industry'. *Transport Reviews* 38(1): 117–38.

Rodrigues, G. and Breach, A. 2021. *Measuring Up: Comparing public transport in the UK and Europe's biggest cities*. London: Centre for Cities.

Robson, E., Wijayaratna, K. and Dixit, V. 2018. 'A review of computable general equilibrium models for transport and their application in appraisal'. *Transportation Research Part A* 116: 31–53.

Ronnie, E. 2017. 'A novel approach to economic evaluation of infrastructure? Examining the benefit analyses in the Swedish high-speed rail project'. *Case Studies on Transport Policy* 5(3): 492–8.

Rupprecht Consult. 2019. *Guidelines for Developing and Implementing a Sustainable Urban Mobility Plan*, second edition. Cologne: Rupprecht Consult.

SACTRA 1994. *Trunk Roads and the Generation of Traffic: Report of the Standing Advisory Committee on Trunk Road Assessment*. London: Department for Transport. https://infrastructure.planninginspectorate.gov.uk/wp-content/ipc/uploads/projects/TR010044/TR010044-001678-sactra-1994-trunk-roads-traffic-report-unlocked.pdf. Accessed 16 February 2024.

SACTRA 1999. *Transport and the Economy: Full report. Report of the Standing Advisory Committee on Trunk Road Assessment*. London: Department for Transport. https://www.ffue.org/wp-content/uploads/2016/08/SACTRA_Full-report.pdf. Accessed 16 February 2024.

Sahlins, M. 1972. *Stone Age Economics* (republished 2017). London: Routledge.

Salutin, G. 2023. *Getting the Measure of Transport Poverty*. London: Social Market Foundation.

Schafer, A. and Victor, D. 2000. 'The future mobility of the world population'. *Transportation Research Part A* 34(3): 171–205.

Scottish Government. 2020. *Securing a Green Recovery on a Path to Net Zero: Climate change plan 2018–2032 – update*. Edinburgh: Scottish Government.

Sharma, R. and Newman, P. 2018. 'Does rail increase land value in emerging cities? Value uplift from Bangalore Metro'. *Transport Research Part A* 117: 70–86.

Sheller, M. 2004. 'Automotive emotions: Feeling the car'. *Theory, Culture and Society* 21(4/5): 221–42.

Silva, C., Bertolini, L., te Brömmelstroet, M., Milakis, D. and Papa, E. 2017. 'Accessibility instruments in planning practice: Bridging the implementation gap'. *Transport Policy* 53: 135–45.

Simmonds, D. 2023. 'Accessibility-based land-use/transport appraisal'. [personal communication]

Sloman, L., Dennis, S., Hopkinson, L., Goodman, A., Farla, K., Hiblin, B. and Turner, J. 2021. *Summary and Synthesis of Evidence: Cycle City Ambition Programme 2013–2018*. London: Department for Transport.

Sloman, L., Hopkinson, L. and Taylor, I. 2017. *The Impact of Road Projects in England*. London: CPRE.

Small, K. 1999. 'Project evaluation'. In J.A. Gomez-Ibanez, W. Tye and C. Winston (eds), *Essays in Transportation Economics and Policy: A handbook in honor of John R. Meyer*, 137–77. Washington, DC: Brookings Institution Press.

Small, K. 2012. 'Valuation of travel time'. *Economics of Transportation* 1 (1–2): 2–14.

Smallwood, N. 2023. Oral evidence: Infrastructure. Q20. House of Commons Treasury Committee. 14 November.

Song, Z., Cao, M., Han, T. and Hickman, R. 2019. 'Public transport accessibility and housing value uplift: Evidence from the Docklands light railway in London'. *Case Studies on Transport Policy* 7(3): 607–16.

STAG. 2022. *Scottish Transport Appraisal Guidance: Managers guide*. Edinburgh: Transport Scotland.

Steg, L. 2005. 'Car use: Lust and must. Instrumental, symbolic and affective motives for car use'. *Transportation Research Part A* 39(2–3): 147–62.

Stokes, G. 2013. 'The prospects for future levels of car access and use'. *Transport Reviews* 33(3): 360–75.

Swinney, P., Graham, D., Vera, O., Anupriya, Hörcher, D. and Ojha, S. 2023. *Office Politics: London and the rise of home working*. London: Centre for Cities.

Tabuchi, T. 2011. 'City formation and transport costs'. In A. de Palma, R. Lindsey, E. Quinet and R. Vickerman (eds), *A Handbook of Transport Economics*, 116–32. Cheltenham: Edward Elgar.

Teixeira, J., Silva, C. and Moura e Sá, F. 2021 'Empirical evidence on the impacts of bikesharing: A literature review'. *Transport Reviews* 41(3): 329–51.

TfL. 2009. *Vauxhall Nine Elms Battersea: Transport study report*. London: Transport for London.

TfL. 2013. *Cycle Superhighways: Board paper, 27 March*. London: Transport for London.

TfL. 2014. *River Crossings Development Study, Task 126: Final report*. London: Transport for London.

TfL. 2017. *Land Value Capture: Final report. Annex 7: Literature review*. London: Transport for London.

TfL. 2019. *Travel in London: Report 12*. London: Transport for London.

TfL. 2021a. *Traffic Modelling Guidelines, Version 4.0*. London: Transport for London.

TfL 2021b. *Financial Stability Plan*. London: Transport for London.

TfL. 2022a. *Travel in London: Report 15*. London: Transport for London.

TfL. 2022b. *Elizabeth Line: Evidencing the value (benefits framework)*. London: Transport for London.

TfL. 2023. *Travel in London 2023: Annual overview*. London: Transport for London.

TfL. (n.d.). *London's Strategic Transport Models*. London: Transport for London.

Thaler, R. 1999. 'Mental accounting matters'. *Journal of Behavioural Decision Making* 12: 183–206.

Thaler, R. 2000. 'From Homo economicus to Homo sapiens'. *Journal of Economic Perspectives* 14(1): 133–41.

Transport Access Manual. 2020. *Transport Access Manual: A guide for measuring connection between people and places*. Committee for the Transport Access Manual. https://transportist.org/transport-access-manual-a-guide-for-measuring-connection-between-people-and-places. Accessed 16 February 2024.

Transport & Environment. 2022. *Roadmap to Climate Neutral Aviation in Europe*. Brussels: Transport & Environment.

Transport for the North. 2022. *Transport-related social exclusion in the North of England*. Manchester: Transport for the North.

Transport Scotland. 2022. *Reducing Car Use for a Healthier, Fairer and Greener Scotland*. Edinburgh: Transport Scotland.

TSGB (continuous series). *Transport Statistics Great Britain*. London: Department for Transport.

Tsoleridis, P., Choudhury, C. and Hess, H. 2022. 'Deriving transport appraisal values from emerging revealed preference data'. *Transportation Research Part A* 165: 225–45.

UITP. 2020. *Full Free Fare Public Transport: Objectives and alternatives*. Brussels: International Association of Public Transport.

Van Essen, M., Thomas, T., Van Berkum, E. and Chorus, C. 2016. 'From user equilibrium to system optimum: A literature review on the role of travel information, bounded rationality and non-selfish behaviour at the network and individual levels'. *Transport Reviews* 36(4): 527–48.

Van Wee, B. 2021a. 'Accessibility and mobility: Positional goods? A discussion paper'. *Journal of Transport Geography* 92: 103033.

Van Wee, B. 2021b. 'Cycling economics'. In Roger Vickerson (ed.), *International Encyclopedia of Transportation* 1: 414–18. Amsterdam: Elsevier.

Venables, A. 2021. 'Wider economic impacts of transport investments'. In Roger Vickerman (ed.), *International Encyclopedia of Transportation* 1: 355–9. Amsterdam: Elsevier.

Venables, A., Laird, J. and Overman, H. 2014. *Transport Investment and Economic Performance: Implications for project appraisal*. London: Department for Transport.

Venter, C. 2016. *Developing a Common Narrative on Urban Accessibility: A transportation perspective*. Washington, DC: Brookings Institution.

Vickerman, R. 2017. 'Beyond cost-benefit analysis: The search for comprehensive evaluation of transport investment'. *Research in Transportation Economics* 63: 5–12.

Vickerman, R. (ed.). 2021. *International Encyclopedia of Transportation*. Amsterdam: Elsevier.

Vij, A. and Dühr, S. 2022. 'The commercial viability of Mobility-as-a-Service (MaaS): What's in it for existing transport operators, and why should governments intervene?'. *Transport Reviews* 42(5): 695–716.

Volker, J., Lee, A. and Handy, S. 2020. 'Induced vehicle travel in the environmental review process'. *Transportation Research Record* 2674(7): 468–79.

Von Thünen, J. 1826. *Der Isolierte Staat in Beziehung auf Landwirtschaft und Nationalokonomie*. [Available in translation: *Von Thünen's 'Isolated State'*, trans. C. Wartenberg. Oxford: Pergamon, 1966.]

Wardman, M., Chintakayala, P. and Heywood, C. 2020. 'The valuation and demand impacts of the worthwhile use of travel time with specific reference to the digital revolution and endogeneity'. *Transportation* 47(3): 1515–40.

Wardman, M. and Lyons. G. 2016. 'The digital revolution and worthwhile use of travel time: Implications for appraisal and forecasting'. *Transportation* 43(3): 507–30.

Wardrop, J. 1952. 'Some theoretical aspects of road traffic research'. *Proceedings of the Institution of Civil Engineers* 1(3): 325–62.

Welsh Government. 2023. *Welsh Government Response to the Roads Review*. https://www.gov.wales/welsh-government-response-roads-review-html. Accessed 16 February 2024.

WelTAG. 2022. *Welsh Transport Appraisal Guidance (WelTAG) 2022: Consultation draft*. Cardiff: Welsh Government.

What Works Centre for Local Economic Growth. 2015. *Evidence Review 7: Transport*. London: What Works Centre for Local Economic Growth.

White, P. 2018. 'Prospects in Britain in the light of the Bus Services Act 2017'. *Research in Transportation Economics* 69: 337–43.

WHO. 2017. *Health Economic Assessment Tool (HEAT) for Walking and cycling*. Geneva: World Health Organization.

Williams, I. and Jahanshahi, J. 2018. *Wider Factors Affecting Long-Term Growth in Rail Travel*. London: Independent Transport Commission.

Wittwer, R., Gerike, R. and Hubrich, S. 2019. 'Peak-car phenomenon revisited for urban areas: Microdata analysis of household travel surveys from five European capital cities'. *Transportation Research Record* 2673(3): 686–99.

Wong, Y. and Hensher, D. 2018. 'The Thredbo story: A journey of competition and ownership in land passenger transport'. *Research in Transportation Economics* 69: 9–22.

Woodcock, J., Givoni., M. and Morgan, A. 2013. 'Health impact modelling of active travel visions for England and Wales using an integrated transport and health impact modelling tool (ITHIM)'. *PLoS ONE* 8(1): e51462.

Worsley, T. 2012. *Rail Demand Forecasting Using the Passenger Demand Forecasting Handbook: On the Move supporting paper 2*. London: RAC Foundation.

Worsley, T. 2014. 'The evolution of London's Crossrail scheme'. In *Major Transport Infrastructure Projects and Economic Development*. ITF Roundtable 154. Paris: International Transport Forum, OECD Publishing.

Worsley, T. 2015. *Ex-Post Assessment of Transport Investments and Policy Interventions: Summary and conclusions of the roundtable*. Discussion Paper 2014:19. Paris: International Transport Forum, OECD Publishing.

Worsley, T. 2021. 'Are megaprojects too transformational for cost-benefit analysis?'. In Roger Vickerman (ed.), *International Encyclopedia of Transportation* 1: 470–5. Amsterdam: Elsevier.

Worsley, T. and Mackie, P. 2015. *Transport Policy, Appraisal and Decision-Making*. London: RAC Foundation.

WSP. 2018. *Latest Evidence on Induced Travel Demand: An evidence review* [for the Department for Transport]. Manchester: WSP and RAND Europe.

WSP. 2020a. *National Transport Model Version 2R Peer Review* [for the Department for Transport]. Bristol: WSP.

WSP. 2020b. *National Transport Model Version 5 Peer Review* [for the Department for Transport]. Bristol: WSP.

WSP. 2022. *Congestion Dependent Values of Time in Transport Modelling: Further PRISM testing*. Hertford: WSP.

WSP. 2023. *Understanding the Requirements and Barriers for Modal Shift: Report for the Climate Change Committee*. London: WSP.

Zahavi, Y. 1974. *Traveltime Budgets and Mobility in Urban Areas: Final report*. FHWA PL 8183. Washington, DC: US Department of Transportation, Federal Highway Administration.

Index

15-minute city 35, 125

A303 (road) 77–8
access 23, 45–7, 52, 66–8, 90–1, 135–6
    diminishing returns 67–8, 91, 136
    increasing with square of speed 8, 23
active travel 71–2, 85, 111, 121, 125
agglomeration 25, 34, 58, 73, 77, 82
air passenger duty 130
airports 79, 145
    Commission 79–80
air quality 10
air travel 11–12, 19, 21, 29, 39, 130, 137
    decarbonisation 12–13
Amsterdam 6
anarchy, price of 141
automated vehicles (AVs) 20

Barcelona 125
benefit–cost ratio (BCR) 13, 60–3, 74, 76, 78,
    82, 85
Berlin 7, 26
bicycle *see* cycling
Birmingham 26, 75
built environment 125
bus 3, 86–7, 124

California 52
Cambridge 119
Carbon Budget Delivery Plan 132
car ownership 8–9, 24
car use 2–3, 7–8, 16–17, 30
    alternatives 124–7
    conflicts with other road users 11
    dependence 4–9, 123–4
    detrimental consequences 9–11
    dominant mode of travel 2, 13
        in London 3, 6
        parked 9
climate change 20, 111, 132–3
Climate Change Committee 131–2
collisions, of vehicles 10–11, 70
COM-B 129
competition 79, 86–7
Computable General Equilibrium (models) 107
congestion, road traffic 9–10, 19, 50, 53, 54–6,
    71, 90, 121, 139, 144
    charging *see* road pricing
self-regulating 10
Copenhagen 5–6, 26, 125–6
coronavirus *see* pandemic

cost–benefit analysis 41, 43, 47, 66, 69–70, 77,
    88–9, 116
cost-effectiveness analysis 83
Crossrail 72–73
cycling 3, 5–6, 19, 38, 126
    electric 19, 126

demand responsive travel (DRT) 126
demographic change 25–8
    in London 25
Department for Energy Security and Net Zero
    (UK) 131
Department for Levelling Up, Housing and
    Communities (UK) 60
digital navigation 21, 50, 100–1, 121–2, 140–3
digital platforms 20, 126
double counting (of benefits) 60

economic development 64–5
Edinburgh 119
electric vehicles (EVs) 20, 112–13, 117–18, 132
    benefits for air quality 10
Elizabeth Line *see* Crossrail
Emission Trading Scheme 115, 130
environmental impacts 69–70, 121
European Union 125, 130
evaluation 73
externalities 69–71, 90

Fleet Street 34
four-stage models 94, 102, 106, 109
fuel cell electric vehicle (FCEV) 114
fuel duty 117–18, 128

Google Maps 142
governance 84–6
Green Book 69, 81
greenfield housing 124
greenhouse gases 70, 111

Hamburg 7
Heathrow (airport) 11, 79–80, 107
Highways England (*see also* National Highways)
    78
housing 63
HS2 (rail route) 19, 74–6, 107

induced traffic 51–4, 90
inequalities 12–13, 56
Integrated Rail Plan 46, 76–7

INDEX   **159**

internal combustion engine vehicle (ICEV) 113, 116–17, 120, 132
International Council on Clean Transportation 131
International Transport Forum (ITF) 5, 41, 46

Johnson, Boris 119
journey purpose 3
Jubilee Line 61
Juncker, Jean-Claude 133

land use 59–64, 91
 and transport interaction (LUTI) (models) 106–7
Livingstone, Ken 119
London 3, 56, 64, 72, 117, 128, 140
 Docklands 59, 61
river crossings 61
Low Traffic Neighbourhoods 11, 121, 128

M1(motorway) 100
M25 (motorway) 99
Madrid 7
Manchester 26, 119
mature networks 137–141
mental accounting 7
Milton Keynes 59
Mobility as a Service (MaaS) 127
mobility difficulty 7
model validation 96–9, 142
Munich 7

National Audit Office 78, 84
National Highways 120
National Infrastructure Commission 62, 64, 77, 82
National Networks Policy Statement 81, 121
National Road Traffic Forecasts 102–3
National Transport Model (NTM) 102, 105, 131
National Travel Survey (UK) (NTS) 1–4, 15–16, 38–9, 53, 102, 105
National Trip End Model (NTEM) 102–4
Net Zero 5, 21, 111, 114–15, 121, 123, 144
Newhaven (E. Sussex) 61
Northern Line 61, 73–4

Office for Budget Responsibility 117
office space 35
optimism bias 97–9, 131

pandemic 31–40, 130
 travel impact in London 32, 36
Paris 26, 125
plug-in hybrid electric vehicle (PHEV) 114
positional goods 24
public transport 28–9, 120, 127

railways 18–19, 87, 104
 crowding 10
 investment 72–7, 121
reliability 49–50
revealed preference (RP) 48
road freight 141
road investment strategy 120
road pricing 55–6, 90, 117–20, 128
road user charging see road pricing

rule-of-a-half 44
rural travel 124

satnav see digital navigation
saturation see travel demand saturation
SATURN (model) 99–100
Scottish government 85, 123, 129
scrappage (of vehicles)120
shared use (of vehicles) 126
shopping 37, 141
Singapore 56, 61, 117, 128
smart motorways 99
smartphones 119
Smeed, Reuben, 56
spatial economics 63–4
speed of travel 19–20
Sports Utility Vehicles (SUVs) 9
stated preference (SP) 48–51, 78
Stockholm 56, 117, 128
Stonehenge 77–8
sustainable aviation fuel (SAF) 123
Sweden 76

Thredbo (conference) 86
TomTom 142
transit-oriented development 125
Transport Analysis Guidance (TAG) 42, 46, 84, 94, 137, 146
Transport Decarbonisation Plan (UK) 111, 121, 126, 131
Transport for London (TfL) 32, 36, 38, 61, 73, 87
transport investment appraisal 43–44
 strategic case 80–83
transport poverty 12
transport technologies 17–22
travel demand saturation 22–5, 67–8, 91, 136–7, 145
travel information 140
travel time 15, 17–18, 21, 30, 36, 121
 budget 45
 invariance 17, 44, 60, 63, 77, 90, 105–7
 saving 41, 43, 46, 56, 85
TUBA (model) 100

Uber 20
Ultra Low Emission Zone (ULEZ) 118

value of travel time (savings) 43, 47–9
 small (time savings) 50–1
Vienna 6–7, 26
Vision Zero 11

walking 3, 126
Wardrop, J. 106, 140–1
Waze 142
Welsh government 82, 85, 121
wider economic impacts 56–9, 73, 79, 91
willingness to pay (WTP) 47, 60, 68, 70, 78
working from home 31–6
workplace parking levy 128
World Health Organization 71

young people, travel behaviour thereof 26–7

zero-emission vehicle mandate 115–16
Zurich 6–7

www.ingramcontent.com/pod-product-compliance
Lightning Source LLC
Chambersburg PA
CBHW071336030525
25994CB00013B/32